SERGE KOUSSEVITZKY

LONDON : GEOFFREY CUMBERLEGE
OXFORD UNIVERSITY PRESS

SERGE KOUSSEVITZKY

serge
koussevitzky

the
boston symphony orchestra
and the new american music

By HUGO LEICHTENTRITT *, 1874-1951*

1947
CAMBRIDGE, MASSACHUSETTS
HARVARD UNIVERSITY PRESS

Second Printing

COMPOSED AND PRINTED BY NORWOOD
PRESS AND BOUND BY STANHOPE BINDERY
IN THE UNITED STATES OF AMERICA

ACKNOWLEDGMENTS

For kind permission to make quotations from copyrighted material the author is indebted to Dr. Serge Koussevitzky, Mr. Olin
Downes, Mr. Robert Lawrence, The New York Times, The Boston Herald, and the management of the Boston Symphony
Orchestra.

CONTENTS

SERGE KOUSSEVITZKY

INTRODUCTION

The history of American music has not yet been written in detail, though many attempts have been made to describe certain phases of it. The present investigation is devoted to perhaps the most important phase of all: the new symphonic music that came into existence mainly through the initiative of Dr. Serge Koussevitzky and the realization of his artistic intentions by the Boston Symphony Orchestra. As will be shown in this survey, American symphonic music probably owes more to the uninterrupted efforts of Dr. Koussevitzky and the Boston Symphony Orchestra than to any other conductor and orchestral group. For more than twenty years, from his first season in Boston, in 1924, to the present time, Koussevitzky has encouraged the development of young native composers and has tested their works through public performances. In so doing, he has rendered an inestimable service to the younger generation of American composers.

His task has not been to choose the most finished compositions of an abundant literature, as would have been the case with the great symphonic works of German, Russian, and French masters. Masterpieces were not abundant in the still young American symphonic art, and severe critics might have questioned whether there were any at all. Had Koussevitzky waited for masterpieces to appear before conducting any new compositions, his roster of first performances would have been meager indeed. His method was to educate inexperienced but gifted young composers by letting them hear their own, often immature, efforts. Thus they could learn where their scores failed to produce the intended effect and could gain priceless experience that would benefit their later works. They could also perceive the reaction of the listening public and the attitude of professional critics of newspapers and magazines. Examining the long list of Koussevitzky's

first performances through the years, one can see how his policy
has raised the standard of American production, how composers
have grown in stature, and how much the present leaders of
American symphonic music have profited in technical skill, artistic ambition, and creative power from constant intercourse with
the Boston Symphony Orchestra and its distinguished conductor.

What Koussevitzky has achieved for modern music by supporting it enthusiastically can be realized more convincingly when
one reads a public statement by the management of the Philadelphia Orchestra on August 28, 1932. It declared that "debatable"
new compositions would not be performed by the orchestra—
an attempt to appease the considerable portion of Philadelphia
music lovers averse to the bold experiments of modernistic music.
Gradually, however, Koussevitzky and the Boston Symphony
Orchestra awakened prominent orchestras from their indiffer-
ence toward new American works. Thus one sees during the
thirties a growing interest in modern works in New York, Chicago, Cleveland, Philadelphia, and other large cities. It is worth
mentioning, too, that Monteux in San Francisco was so liberal
a patron of talented young Americans that a few years ago his
public protested against too many novelties.

The works of American music to be described here represent
only a small cross section of what has actually been composed
in the United States since about 1890. Yet this cross section comprehends many different directions; and it is hoped that it may
serve as a guide through the amazing variety of modern American music. Not many names of real merit are absent from Koussevitzky's programs. But in order that both the scene to be described and the character of its protagonist may gain definition,
it will be helpful to cast a rapid glance at the history of the
Boston Symphony Orchestra and at the artistic evolution of
Serge Koussevitzky.*

* Much of the source material for this discussion appears in the program books of the Boston Symphony Orchestra concerts. Written for
more than thirty years by the scholar and critic Philip Hale, and after
his death by the able and well-instructed John N. Burk, they abound
in valuable and interesting material. The excellent *History of the*

In 1924, when Koussevitzky took over the reins of the Boston Symphony Orchestra, this famous group had already reached its forty-third anniversary. It had been founded in 1881 and sustained most liberally for many years by Major Henry Lee Higginson, a wealthy music enthusiast of Boston. About 1880 symphonic music was just beginning to capture public attention. Only a few major orchestras existed before the new Boston orchestra—the New York Philharmonic–Symphony Orchestra and the various orchestras directed by Theodore Thomas. The Boston Symphony quickly became one of the best, owing to the excellence of its conductors and the virtuoso skill of its carefully chosen members. As Germany was at that time the uncontested home of symphonic music and orchestral playing, the conductors of the new orchestra as well as the majority of its members were German and Austrian. The list of conductors includes eminent, often world-famous, musicians: George Henschel, Wilhelm Gericke, Arthur Nikisch, Emil Paur, Max Fiedler, and Karl Muck, whose second term of office (1913–1918) saw the climax thus far of the Orchestra's artistic efficiency. Unfortunately, the detention of the famous conductor Karl Muck in an American camp in 1918 had a disastrous effect on the Orchestra, with its many German members. A French interregnum was tried to save the situation, and Henri Rabaud (1918–1919) and after him Pierre Monteux did their best to restore the Orchestra. It remained for Koussevitzky, however, to bring the Orchestra back to its former eminence and to lead it to new triumphs.

Serge Koussevitzky, born in Russia in 1874 and educated at

Boston Symphony Orchestra, by M. A. DeWolfe Howe in collaboration with J. N. Burk, has been of great help. And the sixty-odd volumes filled with newspaper clippings—a well-nigh complete collection of the critical reviews of the Orchestra's concerts at home and in other cities —in the Orchestra's library, yielded much valuable material. For the kind permission to use these sources freely and to quote from them extensively, the author is greatly indebted to the management of the Boston Symphony Orchestra. The scores of a number of the compositions performed by the Orchestra and several books concerned with the history of this distinguished orchestral group and the biography of Serge Koussevitzky have also contributed to the author's information.

the Moscow Conservatory, was first known to the world of music after 1900 as a brilliant virtuoso on the double bass. He was heard and admired in many countries and had hardly a rival in his mastery of the huge bass viol, which is not generally considered a solo instrument. Not content with fame thus gained, he aimed at becoming an orchestral conductor, one who would rival the great masters of the baton. Arthur Nikisch, who in the first decade of this century was Europe's most admired and applauded symphonic conductor, was one of Koussevitzky's main inspirations. Nikisch's passionate, improvisatory, rhapsodic manner, and his sensitivity to the magic of colorful sound struck a related chord in the nature of the young Russian musician. Moreover, Nikisch had no superior, in fact hardly a rival, in his rendering of Russian music; in particular he was more responsible than any other conductor for the world celebrity of Tchaikovsky.

It is no wonder that young Koussevitzky was profoundly stirred by Nikisch's art and that it became his ardent desire to achieve something similar. At that time Berlin was the center of the international musical world, and Nikisch was the permanent conductor of the famous concerts of the Berlin Philharmonic Orchestra. Koussevitzky spent some apprentice years there studying the methods of Nikisch and other famous conductors, and he profited from the unexcelled wealth of the city's musical life. Returning to Moscow, he found means in 1909 to establish a new orchestra to be conducted by him. Thus from the start, he was his own boss and has remained so practically all of the time. Though maintaining independence in artistic matters, and though always remaining the leader, he nevertheless has not acted as an autocrat, but has ever considered the best advantage of the cause to which he has devoted his life.

In a few years the excellence of his work in Moscow won him a reputation as one of Russia's best conductors, and about 1910 he had already begun to establish an artistic policy which is still manifest in his Boston activities thirty years later. The great, universally recognized works of symphonic literature were the firm pillars on which he founded his program. Here was the best in existence, offered to his public in finished performances. In addition, he turned his attention in large measure to contemporary production. The new Russian national art that followed Tchaikovsky, Moussorgsky, and Rimsky-Korsakoff owes him a great debt. Scriabin, Glazunoff, Taneieff, Liadoff, Stravinsky especially, and later the younger generation headed by Prokofieff, were again and again brought by him before the public, and their names and music became familiar to Russian music lovers.

In encouraging this national art, Koussevitzky was not content to be active as a conductor in the customary manner. He sought and found novel, unorthodox methods of promotion. One of them was the founding in 1909 of his own publishing house, "L'Édition Russe de Musique," an enterprise in which he was aided by his wife, Mme. Natalie Koussevitzky—a generous, thoughtful collaborator throughout her husband's career. L'Édition Russe was devoted exclusively to new Russian music, which it made easily available in printed form to other countries—Germany, Austria, France, England, Holland, Belgium, and America. This, of course, facilitated foreign performances of recent Russian works. Later, L'Édition Russe was transferred to Paris, and branch offices were maintained in Berlin and other European capitals. The world celebrity of Scriabin, Rachmaninoff, Stravinsky, and Prokofieff is greatly due to the help they received by the publication of practically all their new scores. A similarly comprehensive Edition of New American Music is still lacking; without such an institution many valiant efforts of gifted American composers are doomed to speedy oblivion.

In the same broadminded manner, Koussevitzky was also active as an educator. What he realized a generation later in his Berkshire Music Center was present in mind during those days in Moscow, and only the outbreak of war in 1914 and the Russian Revolution in 1918 prevented him from carrying out his advanced plans for the education of the highly gifted young Russian professional musicians.

Meanwhile, for the masses of the music-loving Russian people, he undertook an enterprise that was and is unique. In those days when radio and records did not exist, the population of the vast provincial areas, enthusiastic as they were for music in a more or less primitive manner, had little or no opportunity to become acquainted with the more pretentious art of music. As Koussevitzky could not bring all these people to Moscow's concert halls, he devised the fantastic plan of carrying music to them. It called for a large expedition to sail with his orchestra down the Volga River nearly a thousand miles to the Caspian Sea. It scheduled stops all along the banks, when symphonic music would be played to the people. Accordingly, a spacious steamer was chartered as conveyance and living quarters for the Koussevitzky party, a number of distinguished guests from foreign countries, and the orchestra. The trip was leisurely, spanning four to six weeks, and it was made several summers. Several Berlin participants in this Volga expedition have given such colorful reports to the author that he has been able to build up in his imagination a modern saga as adventuresome as the Arabian Nights. Koussevitzky's resourcefulness, idealism, and princely hospitality contributed to this highly original plan of a musical expedition. Though its costs were considerable, he fortunately had available funds. But financial risks have never been an impediment to him when an artistic goal has been sufficiently tempting.

This Russian artist was not only nationally minded; at the same time, as an enthusiastic and highly cultured European, he was intensely interested in the modern achievements of other countries. Whatever excited the public in Berlin, Vienna, Paris, London, and Scandinavian cities he imported to Moscow. Thus Koussevitzky became a champion of international modernism in music. The new works of Debussy, Ravel, Richard Strauss, Mahler, Reger, Sibelius, Busoni, and many others were introduced by him to Moscow's public, and in exchange he performed important new Russian works in his concerts in other countries.

Koussevitzky's brilliant career in Russia was brought to a standstill by the first World War and the ensuing revolution. Although he was appointed chief conductor of the Russian State Orchestra (the former Imperial Orchestra) in Petrograd by the provisional government after the first revolution, he found it expedient to leave Russia altogether in 1920 when the Bolshevik government was established. He took up his residence in Paris, founded a new orchestra, which he conducted, and soon infused new blood into the then somewhat anemic body of Parisian music.

His four seasons in Paris, 1920–1924, had influence far beyond the French capital. Koussevitzky's interesting programs, with their numerous novelties from many countries, their exciting impressions, and their artistic finish, gave new luster to the conductor's name. Music lovers in other countries were eager to hear his concerts. In England especially he became a favorite guest conductor of the country's finest orchestras, in London, Manchester, Glasgow, Liverpool, Edinburgh, and other cities. In Berlin, Rome, Barcelona, Madrid, Lisbon, Warsaw, and other places he was also welcomed as a symphonic conductor of the first rank. While in Paris, Barcelona, and Lisbon, he brought out a number of Russian operas by Moussorgsky, Borodin, Tchaikovsky, and Rimsky-Korsakoff.

Approaching his fiftieth year, Koussevitzky had now attained full mastery of his art, full maturity of interpretation, full control of his individual style. After the death of Nikisch he had a greater international prestige than any other contemporary conductor. It seems logical that therefore the trustees of the Boston Symphony Orchestra chose him in preference to any other conductor when, in 1924, they had the urgent responsibility of reorganizing the Boston Symphony Orchestra under a leader of unsurpassed authority, great renown, and fascinating personality.

The Great War had finished the era of German predominance in the best American orchestras. After the unfortunate events accompanying Karl Muck's exit from the Boston Symphony Orchestra there was little inclination in 1923 to invite another German conductor. Just at that time the pernicious inflation period had been overcome in Germany. The country began to revive, and music and drama quickly regained much of their former brilliance. Moreover, the Hitler regime was still a decade distant, and in 1924 the eminent German conductors were not possessed of the burning desire to emigrate to America that hit them in 1933. Under these conditions the choice of Koussevitzky was the ideal solution of a knotty and difficult problem. The Boston Symphony Orchestra and Koussevitzky almost seem to have been destined for each other, and their union constitutes one of the most satisfying and captivating chapters in the history of American music. The uninterrupted collaboration of the Orchestra and its new conductor for more than twenty years is also of prime importance, inasmuch as it stabilized the novel artistic policies and ideals of Koussevitzky and helped to give them not only a local but also a nation-wide field of action. Only the Chicago Symphony Orchestra and its former conductor Frederick Stock may claim a longer period of continuous collaboration.

As the present investigation is concerned with American music, it becomes necessary to explain what is meant by the term. At first sight a definition seems to be superfluous. One speaks of Italian, German, French, and Russian music, and everyone knows what is meant without lengthy discussion. Why should not the same be true of American music? A closer inspection, however, will easily reveal how different the situation of American music is from that of the music of European countries. Music in America is not an old but rather a young institution. It is not based on any one well-defined national musical substance but is a compound of influences and importations from many countries. Only during the last twenty-five years or so has a clearly perceptible national American music evolved; it is hardly possible to define it in clear, brief words. Modern American music remains a compound of many ingredients, and the famous "melting pot" theory must necessarily be applied.

Not much more than seventy-five years ago a group of Boston composers, John Knowles Paine, Arthur William Foote, George Whitefield Chadwick, and a little later, Edward Alexander MacDowell and Horatio Parker, laid the foundations for an American art of music. Though they all were of New England stock, their music reëchoed the German idiom so strongly that an American flavor is only rarely and faintly perceptible. In the nineties, Antonin Dvořák came to America, and called the attention of American composers to the songs and dances of the Negroes and the Indians. A generation later this prophetic work of the great Bohemian musician gave a new impetus to American music. The music of the Indians was also explored in the early years of our century, owing to the advance of the new science of comparative musicology. Practical results of this research appear in MacDowell's "Indian Suite," in many compositions of Charles Wakefield Cadman, the specialist in Indian music, and Ferruccio Busoni's "Indianische Fantasie." When the large orchestras in New York, Boston, Chicago, Philadelphia, Cincinnati, Saint Louis, and other cities were founded, they brought along an influx of foreign, mainly German, musicians, some of whom were respectable, even outstanding, composers. Thus from the ranks of the Boston Symphony Orchestra emerged such composers as Charles M. Loeffler, Henry Eichheim, and Gustav Strube.

After World War I the first wave of Americanism invaded European countries—the jazz music that owes its vitality not to the white American musicians but to the exciting and orgiastic rhythms and the burlesque, distorted melodies of the Negroes. Jazz, however, was the music of the dance halls and variety shows and did not gain access to the symphony halls for many years. Gradually jazz was refined and artistically exploited by talented white musicians. But again we see in the front ranks not the Americans of old stock but the descendants of Jewish immigrants, mainly from Poland and Russia, with the highly gifted George Gershwin as the leading personality. In the twenties, elements of jazz were incorporated into symphonic music, and thus one characteristic feature of a real American style was established. Another characteristic feature was added when the wealth of American folksongs and dance tunes was explored, thanks to the efforts of the scientists of folklore. Here at last was a musical substance, truly characteristic of this continent. In the symphonies of Roy Harris we see the most accomplished application so far of this new folklore movement.

Negro spirituals and dance tunes and American folk music represent only a raw material of the new American music. A supple and elaborate symphonic technique is needed in order to achieve something impressive with any sort of thematic material. The older New England school had been brought up on the German classical and romantic symphonic technique. After World War I the young American composers usually went to Paris for further study, where most of them were pupils of Nadia Boulanger. In Paris they did not, of course, learn what to do about a national American school of composition, but came under the strong influence of Debussy, Ravel, and Stravinsky in his Parisian phase. In the meantime the musical situation in America kept constantly changing in consequence of Europe's troubles. The Russian Revolution brought many fine musicians as refugees to America; ten years later the Hitler scourge drove many others here, fugitives from Germany, Austria, Italy, France, Poland, Czechoslovakia, Hungary, Belgium. Consequently, there is at present a unique spectacle on the American scene. The shining lights of European music have settled in the United States, where they have been welcomed and cordially invited to continue their important creative work. Stravinsky, Rachmaninoff, Schönberg, Hindemith, Milhaud, Bartók, Bloch, Martinu, Křenek, Toch, Weill, and Castelnuovo-Tedesco, as well as other well-known European celebrities, artists of widely differing tendencies, became active in America, creating new works and teaching and influencing young American composers in many diverging directions.

These masters with their well-founded reputations and their settled artistic principles have remained essentially what they were before. They neither wished nor were they able to transform themselves into American artists, though they welcomed American citizenship. But they have influenced American musical life strongly by both their old and new works, which constantly appear on American programs, and by their teaching. Thus, though not being American in their creative activity, they are an important force in America's musical life. It is not surprising that Koussevitzky, a conductor of universal tendencies, should welcome most of these foreign composers in his programs.

The present investigation, however, is not concerned primarily with these older masters but rather with their American pupils. In them rests the hope for a truly American style of composition. The problem of these younger men is not easy to solve. They have now become conscious of their American spirit, they are determined to establish an American style of serious music far above the already worn-off sensations of jazz. In their endeavor to acquire a brilliant technique of symphonic composition they must find their way through a maze of foreign methods: Stravinsky's neo-classicism, Schönberg's twelve-tone system, Hindemith's contrapuntal virtuosity, Milhaud's polytonality, and so on. They have to absorb what is fitting for them, reject what is contrary to their nature. They have to acquire a novel style of harmony and counterpoint, a formal constructive system that is modern, without closely imitating the manner of their foreign, un-American masters. They have to adapt their newly learned technical skill to the newly consolidated, typically American thematic material, and finally they have to evolve distinct individuality. In the ranks of these young aspirants for national honors there are a number of native Americans, but still more are immigrants or sons of immigrants from Russia, Poland, Hungary, Germany, Italy, and other countries. Some of mixed origin have succeeded in Americanizing themselves to such a degree that they have become potent forces in the evolution of a truly American school of composition. The predominance of Jewish talent in this new American art of music is one remarkable feature.

This, in a general outline, is the present picture of music in America. In the following survey of Koussevitzky's support of new American music, in the twenty-odd years from 1924 to 1946, this summary sketch will be filled in more in detail. This discussion may contribute to a clarification of the aims and methods of new American music. Yet it cannot sufficiently appraise the achievements of Dr. Koussevitzky. They comprise, besides his efforts in behalf of a national American school and his aims as an educator, his important interest in what happens in the international field and his activities as an interpreter of the great masters of the past.

CHAPTER 2

KOUSSEVITZKY'S FIRST
SEASONS IN BOSTON

The news that Koussevitzky had accepted the call to Boston caused a great deal of excitement and speculation in the musical circles not only of Boston but of New York and other cities. On May 5, 1924, the *New York Telegram* reported on the "dynamic Russian," the "Lightning Conductor," as he was called in London. Olin Downes sent to the *New York Times* (June 15, 1924) a long article from Paris, entitled "Koussevitzky as a Magnetic Personality." He calmed the fears of Boston music lovers that Koussevitzky might give them "programs of the extremely brilliant and ultra-modern quality that he has been giving this spring in Paris. Koussevitzky has been told that Americans do not like too much pepper where orchestral music is concerned and he is inclined to be cautious in this direction." Koussevitzky as "a storm center" was enthusiastically described. In many papers appeared his assertion that he was just as much interested in the classics as in modern works—evidently the Bostonians had grave doubts in that respect. They should have read Ernest Newman's "Koussevitzky" article in the September issue of the *American Mercury,* in which the famous British critic extolled the Russian conductor as a great master of the German classic style, explaining at length why Koussevitzky's rendering of Beethoven's Ninth Symphony was superior to that of Weingartner, and that the true Beethoven became alive in Koussevitzky's genuinely classic reading. In an article "As the Door Swings Open Upon Music," Boston's well-known critic H. T. Parker prepared his readers in the *Transcript* of September 6, 1924, for the arrival of the impatiently expected conductor: "a public that is to be thrice blessed in the coming of a conductor of the first rank in both Western and Eastern Europe: a classicist, a romanticist and a modernist justly and discerningly fused." Some American papers

consoled the public by asserting again and again that Koussevitzky "calls jazz music good." Others declared that Koussevitzky
emphatically denied he would "shock cultured Bostonians" by
including jazz in his programs.

At last the great day arrived. Dozens of journalists reported
Koussevitzky's landing at New York, and his arrival in Boston
on September thirteenth. The *Boston Herald* was confident that
Koussevitzky "won't shock music lovers" by giving them "undiluted modernism." And articles from many American papers—
collected in Boston's Symphony Hall—tell of the sensation-laden
atmosphere in Boston that September.

After this tremendous press barrage came the explosion—the
first concert, on October 10, 1924. The public's reaction was com-
mensurate with the loud preparation. Koussevitzky's first appearance with the Boston Symphony Orchestra was considered a
major event in America's cultural life and was treated accordingly in the press of Boston, New York, and many other
cities.

The programs of a conductor's first season in a foreign country
and before a new public are always revealing. They reflect not
only his own taste but also his endeavors to get in close touch
with his public, either by yielding to its habits and preferences
or by trying to reform its taste. Koussevitzky's first Boston program was evidently the result of careful reflection. The first part
was a respectful tribute to the familiar, classical masters Vivaldi,
Berlioz, and Brahms. Next followed a short novelty that in the
twenties had produced a sensation in Europe, Honegger's "Pacific 231." In its title and its character this brilliant, effective,
and up-to-date score concerning a giant locomotive meant a
compliment to American technical efficiency and vitality. The
entire second part of the program was given over to an eminent
modern Russian work, Scriabin's "Poème de l'extase." Koussevitzky presented this work with truly sovereign power, infusing
it with qualities of his Russian temperament, passionate, un-
bridled eruptions as well as depths of melancholy and despair.
Those in the audience old enough to remember Arthur Nikisch
in Boston, thirty years back, might have felt that Koussevitzky

was the legitimate successor of that weird romantic magician of the orchestra.

In the press notices there was consensus that the new conductor had fulfilled, even surpassed, all expectations in the standard classical pieces of his program. Discussion was mainly concerned with the two modern pieces. Olin Downes in his report to the *New York Times* wrote that with the "Poème de l'extase" Koussevitzky "swept his audience from its feet." Philip Hale (*Boston Herald*, October 11) praised the performance of the "Poème," but was not enthusiastic about the piece itself, which he called "hysterical, with its theosophically Wagnerian pages." Hale also had reservations about Honegger's "Pacific 231." The piece, he wrote, "is amusing, it even gives the hearer what Athenaeus said was one of music's missions, 'a gentleman-like joy.' No doubt this music of Honegger is clever, but cleverness in music quickly palls." Almost all other reviews agreed in their interest in Honegger's musical apotheosis of a giant locomotive, which appealed to American enthusiasm for engines and technical feats. H. T. Parker (*Transcript*, October 14) gave the most imaginative and at the same time precise account in his paragraph "From Postchaise to 'Pacific'":

No musician may hear without admiration the close-knit facture, the unflagging flow of the music, the equal economy and adaptation of means to ends. . . . His measures chortle when the big engine at last heaves itself under way. Soon it is in full flight: while as it grinds along, the music sets it, Kipling-wise, to singing a brief and broken song—say of the zest of might and speed steel-shod.

And with what a flourish "Pacific" ends! Here is the old "grand finale" condensed and concentrated into a dozen measures. . . . A post-chaise crosses music of both Bach and Beethoven. Honegger, still living, prefers the locomotive.

"Pacific" was a great success in America, and Koussevitzky, who had introduced the piece in Europe as well as in America, had made a happy choice by including it in his first program. The piece, loudly acclaimed in Boston, showed the dreaded radical modernism in a favorable light, and Koussevitzky gained credit as a promoter of modernism. Olin Downes (*New York Times*, November 1, 1924) said: "The people wanted to hear the 'locomotive,' and even blasé critics, troubled by many concerts, did leg work so that they might arrive on time to describe the much advertised tone-picture to an expectant public."

Looking over the list of programs in the new conductor's first season, 1924–1925, one can perceive that Koussevitzky cautiously tested his ground with regard to American music. Manifestly he was not yet acquainted with a large number of American works. In the music centers of Europe, American music, even in the mid-twenties, was not considered outstanding enough to be taken over into the symphonic repertory. The exception was MacDowell's Second Piano Concerto, which appeared on continental programs once in a while, and this because the world-famous piano virtuoso Teresa Carreño liked to play it and to gain favor for the composer. In Koussevitzky's Paris and London programs neither new nor older American scores had found a place. However, an observer acquainted with Koussevitzky's artistic attitude might have predicted that he would turn his attention to American productions as soon as he had settled definitely in the new country. National as well as international obligations had always been a major part of Koussevitzky's artistic creed. In Russia he had been champion of new Russian music; during his four Paris seasons he had surveyed contemporary French production and had included in his programs virtually all new works of special distinction; and new German, Italian, and English orchestral scores of especial interest were an inherent part of his concerts.

The twenty-four programs of Koussevitzky's first Boston season list six American compositions. Of these, as will be seen later, the conductor fully identified himself with only one, Aaron Copland's Symphony for Organ and Orchestra. Two other American works were repetitions of familiar compositions heard frequently in Boston in former years, Arthur Foote's Suite for String Orchestra and Loeffler's "La Bonne Chanson." Two others were conducted by their composers. Henry Hadley, guest conductor at a pair of concerts, was evidently responsible for the program that included his Symphony No. 4, "North, East, South and West," dating back as far as 1911, and Henry Eichheim, who for twenty years had been a member of the Boston Symphony Orchestra, conducted his work, "A Chinese Legend."

The first new American piece heard in Koussevitzky's initial season was Edward Burlingame Hill's Scherzo for two pianos and orchestra. It is easy to see that for the choice of this piece two soloists, Guy Maier and Lee Pattison, had been responsible. Famous at that time as a two-piano team, these artists occupied the major part of the program with three works heard for the first time in Boston—Philipp Emanuel Bach's Concerto for two pianos, a new Double Concerto by the English composer Arthur Bliss, written expressly for Maier and Pattison, and Hill's Scherzo. The latter piece, originally written for one piano, had been remodeled for two pianos at the suggestion of the players. Evidently Koussevitzky was much pleased with Hill's music on this occasion. The distinguished Harvard professor of music was already well known to Boston audiences through a number of older works.

Before making any radical innovations Koussevitzky took his time, waiting until he had gained the full sympathies and confidence of his Boston public. Not until the fifth month of his first season did he introduce another of those ultra-modern pieces of which the Boston public was so much afraid. Then, on February 20, 1925, Koussevitzky performed an unknown, untried score by twenty-four-year-old Aaron Copland. This date, important in the history of American music, marks the beginning of a new period—one with which Koussevitzky is inseparably linked. The other five American works heard in Koussevitzky's first Boston season belonged to composers who were older men with more or less established reputations. In the case of Copland, an unknown young American musician, a beginner in symphonic music, was for the first time admitted into the sacred precincts of the Boston Symphony Orchestra.

Aaron Copland himself has told the story of his first meeting with Koussevitzky in Paris, 1923, in "Serge Koussevitzky and the American Composer," published in the *Musical Quarterly* (July 1944) on the occasion of Koussevitzky's seventieth birthday. Nadia Boulanger one day called on Koussevitzky in Paris and introduced her young American pupil Copland, who was carrying a score under his arm. Although Koussevitzky had for many years been accustomed to insistent young visitors menacing him with orchestral scores, this was probably the first time a young American musician had thus invaded his private quarters. The presence of Nadia Boulanger, who was highly respected in Paris, must have eased the embarrassment of this interview for her pupil. Since it had just been publicly announced that Koussevitzky had accepted the call to Boston, Nadia Boulanger had shrewdly concluded that he would be inclined to make the acquaintance of a talented young American. She proved to be correct. Koussevitzky in a jovial mood consented to hear young Copland play part of some recently composed ballet music that he had brought with him. He not only took an interest in the piece but also promised to put it on one of his first Boston programs. The sixteenth Boston program shows the fulfillment of the promise, and young Copland bowed to the Boston public, acknowledging its vigorous applause. A substitution, however, had been made. Instead of the ballet music, Koussevitzky conducted Copland's Symphony for Organ and Orchestra. This new score gave Copland's teacher, Nadia Boulanger, also an expert organist, the welcome opportunity to appear before an American audience.

The Boston papers had much to say on Copland's debut as a composer. The *Globe* (February 21) had as its headline "Copland's Organ Symphony Clapped and Hissed," but Philip Hale, in his review in the *Herald* (February 21), called the audience to order:

A good many were yesterday shocked by this symphony; perhaps affronted, regarding it as a personal insult to subscribers eager to hear music that they knew and liked. Yes, there are some, and they are voluble, who resent the putting of unfamiliar works on Symphony programs. They have no curiosity about what is going on in the musical world. They have ears, but they do not hear, and they are unwilling to hear, unless the new composition is by a local composer with whom they have at least a bowing acquaintance.

Hale thanked Koussevitzky for introducing new works "even if they are apparently ugly at first hearing." He called the symphony an honest work, "though some may with equal honesty think this talent is here misguided." In spite of "pages that are noise, not sound; of acid harmonies that have not the saving grace of exciting surprise, that leave the hearer indifferent or bored," Hale found that the Prelude "in the nature of a reverie has decided character . . . here the composer is simplest and most effective." He pointed to the Stravinsky idol towering "in the musical cathedral," adding, "many are the young worshippers." And he summed up his impression that in Copland's symphony "there is much brass, there is clay; but there is also something of fine silver, if not a little gold."

The *Post* cried out emphatically in its headline, "Barbaric Music—Copland's Work Brutal." The piece was called "disturbing," lacking in "salient musical ideas." Yet the critic at least acknowledged that in "the harsh final movement" there was "a suggestion of force and of power," adding that Copland "in writing has looked not only in his heart, but also in the score of Stravinsky's 'Sacre du Printemps.'" Of all reviewers, Parker (in the *Transcript,* February 21) showed by far the greatest sympathy to Copland. He too praised the Prelude. The Scherzo interested him greatly: "Dissonances sharpen; complexities of thematic treatment as of rhythm, increase. Sense of riot, of fury pervades it. We begin to look to 'Le Sacre' for sources of material." Yet in spite of this dependence on Stravinsky the critic saw some "original device" in the piece. In the Finale he pointed out the Stravinsky vocabulary: "There is every known device for stimulating and overstimulating already high-strung nerves." Yet "we were on the verge of dullness" in occasional moments, when all these "dissonances and rhythmic furies failed to stimulate." In spite of all objections he came to the conclusion that Copland had written "a masterpiece of logical formal construction," but he asked "whether it was worth the doing in the terms and with the language that he uses." And finally observed: "A new piece in these proportions . . . demands nothing short of a new idiom," which evidently is lacking. All reviews agreed in pointing out Stravinsky's "Sacre" as the source of Copland's manner of writing—not then recognized as his own style.

CHAPTER 3

TWO OLDER GENERATIONS
OF AMERICAN COMPOSERS

After the first shock of American modernism administered to his Boston public, Koussevitzky found it expedient to practice restraint and to wait a considerable time before renewing the attack. All the other American works of his first season were decidedly more palatable; compositions by well-known, trusted, older men. Among these familiar musicians whose works Koussevitzky selected for performance were Foote, Loeffler, Hadley, Chadwick, and MacDowell. Members of the older generation of American composers, they had relations with Koussevitzky's work that are worth substantial study.

Arthur Foote, who died in 1937 at the age of eighty-four, was for a long time the highly respected dean of American composers. He belongs to a musical era on which our modernistic age looks back somewhat condescendingly. Yet at least one of his works has a fair chance of becoming an American classic: that serene and beautiful E major Suite for String Orchestra which Koussevitzky inherited from his predecessors and which he has repeated a number of times in later years.

The Koussevitzky programs contain only one piece by Foote besides the E major Suite, "Night Piece" for flute and string orchestra. This unpretentious but charming work—Foote called it "a slight little thing"—written back in 1918 for the Chamber Music Society in San Francisco, has been played four times by Georges Laurent, the excellent solo flutist of the Boston Symphony Orchestra: once in 1921 and once in 1923, and under Koussevitzky's direction on March 10, 1933, and April 16, 1937. Between 1887 and 1939 ten different works of Foote are listed in the Boston Symphony concerts, with a total of twenty performances, inclusive of repetitions.

Charles Martin Loeffler (1861–1935), eight years younger than

Foote, was in the first quarter of our century considered a daring modernist, and his orchestral works were played in Europe as well as in America. Though he spent the greater part of his life in Boston and more than twenty years as second concertmaster of the Boston Symphony Orchestra, he can be called an American composer only with reservations, and he probably never considered himself a representative of American music. An Alsatian by birth, educated partly in Berlin, partly in Paris, he also spent some years of his youth in Russia where he came directly under the spell of Russian music. His music, reflecting German, modern French, and Russian influences, is a unique blend, combining German structural solidity with French impressionistic refinement of color, and having Russian reminiscences in its predilection for modal harmony and in certain melodic features.

Koussevitzky has shown respect for Loeffler's art by performing in the course of time half a dozen of his representative works. Since Loeffler's death, in 1935, growing interest in works of younger Americans has diverted attention from Loeffler's achievements. Yet this oblivion, one may well believe, is only temporary. Scores with such substantial contents and elaborate and interesting symphonic technique as "A Pagan Poem," "La Mort de Tintagiles," and others belong with the most representative products of their age and are bound to regain the attention due their quality.

For the season 1925–1926 Koussevitzky selected a new score by Loeffler that had recently been awarded a thousand-dollar prize by the Chicago North Shore Festival Association and had been performed in quick succession at Evanston, Chicago, Cleveland, and New York. This symphonic poem, "Memories of My Childhood," must have had particular appeal to Koussevitzky, for in it Loeffler tells in musical terms the story of happy boyhood years spent in a Russian village. In his preface to this score, Loeffler speaks of the distant church bells; the Russian peasant songs; the litany melody "God Have Mercy Upon Us"; and the dance with the rustic accompaniment by four mouth harmonicas, clarinet, and piccolo flute alternating with the violas in the presentation of the tune.

In 1927–1928 Koussevitzky conducted one of Loeffler's principal works, "A Pagan Poem," Opus 14. This composition, inspired by Vergil's eighth Eclogue (called the Sorceress), had originally been conceived as a piece of chamber music. Later transformed into an orchestral work, the score became so effective that the Boston Symphony Orchestra performed it no less than eight times, a distinction accorded very few other works. Four of these performances took place, in 1927, 1935, 1938, and 1943, the first two conducted by Koussevitzky, the last two by concertmaster Richard Burgin, the eminent violinist and associate conductor. Two distinguished members of the Orchestra played the solo parts; Bernard Zighera, the harpist, took the piano part, and Louis Speyer the English horn solo.

Loeffler's "Canticum Fratris Solis" for voice and orchestra was performed by Koussevitzky on January 3, 1930. This famous hymn to "Brother Sun" by St. Francis of Assisi was composed by Loeffler on a modern Italian version rather than on the original in medieval Umbrian dialect. The piece had been written in 1925 in response to Mrs. Elizabeth Sprague Coolidge's invitation and was first heard at the inauguration of the concert hall presented to the Washington Library of Congress by Mrs. Coolidge, generous patroness of chamber music in America. At this performance, as well as several years later in Boston, the Danish singer Povla Frijsh was the soloist. The Boston program book reprints the useful analytical notes written by Lawrence Gilman for the Philadelphia performance in 1926. The score is written with Loeffler's characteristic subtlety of orchestral color, and it abounds in picturesque tonal illustrations of the words used by St. Francis in praise and thanks to the Lord for "our mother the earth—our sister water—our brother wind—our brother fire—our sister death." The hymn's liturgic Gregorian motives are impressively used, particularly for listeners who know and recognize these plain-chant melodies wherever they occur. The combination of a soprano solo voice with a chamber orchestra of three flutes, English horn, two horns, piano, celesta, two harps, organ, and strings is productive of rare sonorities, chosen for special effects by Loeffler--who had an extraordinarily sensitive ear.

Koussevitzky's performance of Loeffler's "La Mort de Tintagiles" on February 26, 1932, was the fulfillment of an artistic duty. This work had not been heard in Boston since 1923, though between that date and 1898 it had seven performances by the Orchestra. Certainly it is one of the most distinguished compositions ever written in America, though one can hardly call it American music. It was inspired by Maeterlinck's little drama for marionettes. An abstract of the sinister, tragic story appears in Philip Hale's program. To enjoy Loeffler's music, however, one does not have to be familiar with all details of the story. The score—not an illustration of the drama scene by scene but of features favorable for musical treatment—makes use of some scenic directions effectively translatable into musical terms. This is certainly program music, but it is also impressionistic music and can be understood, too, as music per se. In fact, it meets the test of excellence. Strange, suggestive, and acoustically charming sonorities abound in this score. Jean Lefranc, solo violist of the Orchestra, played the composition's important viola d'amore part.

The last new work of Loeffler conducted by Koussevitzky was "Evocation," heard on March 31, 1933, and on February 23, 1934. Since Loeffler's death, only a few of his older works have been performed in Symphony Hall. "Evocation," for orchestra, women's chorus, and a speaking voice was written by Loeffler for the dedication of Cleveland's concert hall, Severance Hall, in 1931. The texts were taken from the famous collection of ancient Greek epigrams known as the Greek Anthology. The selection made by Loeffler is renewed proof of his scholarly mind, cultivated literary taste, and understanding of the ancient spirit. This score is one of the noblest and most exalted pieces of music ever written in America, though it is miles distant from the new American trend and in its aristocratic attitude the opposite of popular. The underlying idea is an evocation of music. Pan, god of the nymphs, is invited to play on his pipe under the "stone-pine that murmurs so honey-sweet as it bends to the soft western breeze. . . . Breathe music, O Pan . . . with thy sweet lips, breathe delight into thy pastoral reed." Further on the mythical

"singing stone"—on which Phoebus Apollo had once "laid down
. . . his Delphic harp"—emits its mysterious, fascinating sounds.
The Boston program book quotes a lengthy letter from Loeffler
on the contents and meaning of his "Evocation," a precious document for an understanding of the aesthetic refinement of Loeffler's art. In the Boston performance the Cecilia Society Chorus,
conducted by Arthur Fiedler, participated.

Henry K. Hadley (1871–1937), ten years younger than Loeffler, had for nearly thirty years been America's best-known and
most successful composer and conductor. His numerous orchestral works, symphonies, overtures, tone-poems, choral works,
chamber music, and operas were continually heard and published. As Hadley was born in the close vicinity of Boston and
had been a pupil of Chadwick at the New England Conservatory
before going to Vienna for further studies, it was quite natural
that he had close connection with the Boston Symphony Orchestra. His works appeared eight times in the Boston programs
before Koussevitzky's arrival and three times later, always conducted by the composer. This might indicate a polite gesture by
Koussevitzky to his conductor-colleague, Hadley, but it might also
indicate that the Hadley scores were not sufficiently attractive to
the Boston conductor for him to include them in his own concerts.
Only after the composer's death did Koussevitzky conduct one
of his works: the Andante movement from Hadley's Third Symphony played as a memorial at the Berkshire Festival of 1938.
He repeated the piece a few weeks later at the first Boston
concert of the season 1938–1939. Hadley's last appearance in
Boston as a composer and conductor occurred on January 16,
1931, when he presented his tone-poem "Salomé," Opus 55, and
the suite "Streets of Pekin." The composer stressed the fact that
his "Salomé" score, published in Berlin in 1906, had been composed in Paris before the first performance of Richard Strauss's
opera *Salome* in Dresden, December 9, 1905, and before Hadley
had any acquaintance with the music of Strauss. He thus defended himself against the possible charge of imitating Strauss
or competing with him. Yet the fact that he based his work, as
did Strauss, on Oscar Wilde's drama *Salomé* makes a comparison

of the two compositions inevitable, even if one concedes that Hadley did not intend to compete with Strauss and did not invite such a comparison. No matter how interesting Hadley's score may be, it is a misfortune that it must stand comparison with the inflamed, overpowering, sensational, and unique *Salome* music of Strauss. Indeed, not only Hadley but also all other composers of the Salome story, including Massenet, Antoine Mariotte, Florent Schmitt, Gabriel Pierné, and Glazunoff, are victims of such a comparison.* The same unequal competition, of course, prevails in the case of Debussy and all other Pelléas and Mélisande composers.

In the suite "Streets of Pekin," Hadley joins company with half a dozen or more American composers who revel in musical illustrations of exotic, oriental scenery. The Pekin suite, one of Hadley's latest works, was written in 1930, and owes its existence to Hadley's engagement as guest conductor of the Tokyo New Symphony Orchestra. Its first performance, conducted by the composer, took place in Tokyo, September 24, 1930. The score was dedicated to Viscount or Prince Hidemaro Konoye,† a grandee of the empire, to whom more than to anybody else was due the introduction to Japan of European music, conductors, virtuosos, and expert teachers. The suite consists of seven short sketches: "Great Stone Man's Street—Sweet Rain Street—Ricksha Boy No. 309 (Ma Ben)—Jade Street (Moonlight)—Shoemakers' Street—Sleeping Lotuses—The Forbidden City."

The unparalleled success of Hadley in America during his lifetime gave way to neglect after his death in 1937. Rarely does one nowadays encounter his name on concert programs. More robust leaders of the younger generation have shoved aside Henry

---

* Those interested in the Salome story in world literature will find Philip Hale's comment in the January 16, 1931, Boston program book a most informative and exhaustive essay on this topic.

† The author well remembers Prince Konoye in Berlin, conducting the Philharmonic Orchestra and presenting some of his own compositions in European style. What a change in the international relations in one decade, from the thirties to the forties! A composition based on an American composer's reminiscences of the Chinese capital, Pekin, performed in Tokyo!

Hadley, the representative of a past phase of American music, champion of prize-winners, and favorite of music clubs. Yet a small selection of the rather too abundant and facile output of this extraordinarily talented musician should be remembered.

George W. Chadwick (1854–1931), active in Boston as director of the New England Conservatory during Koussevitzky's first years, was then, together with Arthur Foote, the senior of American musicians. The hold that he once had on the Boston Symphony Orchestra and the appeal he had for the Boston public are indicated in the program book of April 25, 1930; it lists no less than thirty-one performances of Chadwick's works from 1883 until 1930. No other American composer comes even close to this number. Chadwick's numerous works, mostly written many years ago, were characteristic of the earlier phase of American music and did not seem to fit with the greatly changed music of the twenties. Even so they were performed occasionally and were welcomed by conservative listeners on account of a certain straightforward, unproblematic quality, and exuberant melodiousness.

When Chadwick in 1914 wrote "Tam O'Shanter," illustrative of Robert Burns's ballad, his musical description of a Scotch witches' Sabbath must have appeared to him as the acme of boldness. The piece was revived by Koussevitzky on April 22, 1927. One may grant the musicianly technique here displayed, yet feel that the conscientious Yankee Chadwick was inadequate for a task requiring the fiery imagination and virtuosity of a Berlioz, Liszt, Moussorgsky, or Richard Strauss. In playing Chadwick's works occasionally Koussevitzky performed a local duty, paying a compliment to an esteemed and meritorious Boston musician, but one can hardly assume that he was greatly interested in his self-imposed task.

In 1930 fifty years had elapsed since Chadwick's first public appearance as a composer and conductor in Boston. In honor of the distinguished veteran musician Koussevitzky put on his program of April 25, 1930, Chadwick's Sinfonietta in D major, a work dating back to 1904. Its four movements show Chadwick's solid musicianship and evince a certain popular appeal. Between

1930 and 1945, however, the name of Chadwick appears only twice in the Boston programs. After his death on April 4, 1931, he was quickly and thoroughly forgotten. Shortly afterwards, on April 21, 1931, Koussevitzky performed the "Nöel" from Chadwick's "Symphonic Sketches," in memory of the deceased American master. The "Symphonic Sketches," written in 1908, had in previous years been heard three times at Boston Symphony concerts. At this writing the last Chadwick composition heard at Symphony Hall was the "Melpomene" overture, certainly one of his best and without any doubt his most successful and popular work. It was played on February 20, 1942, in a concert conducted by Richard Burgin. The example of Chadwick shows better than any other the powerful effect of a change of taste. It severed his generation from its successor, and its successor in turn from the still younger, third generation that dominates the present age.

Edward MacDowell (1861–1908), though much more up-to-date than Chadwick, was also receding into the background in the mid-twenties. Between 1924 and 1945 his name appears only three times on Boston Symphony programs. In April 1927 Koussevitzky performed one movement of MacDowell's Indian Suite, Opus 48, entitled "In War Time." MacDowell's Second Piano Concerto in D minor, one of his principal works and the only American composition well known in European concert halls, had five performances in Symphony Hall between 1889 and 1924. In Koussevitzky's programs it occurred once, on December 18, 1936, when Howard Goding played the solo part.

The only other revival of a MacDowell score by Koussevitzky took place December 9, 1932, when "Two Poems for Orchestra: Hamlet and Ophelia" was performed. Aside from this, it has never been repeated since the first Boston performance on January 27, 1893. The work is dedicated to the great English actors Henry Irving and Ellen Terry. MacDowell had been deeply moved by their *Hamlet* performance in London, in 1884. Though the printed score carries the title "Two Poems," the composer later changed the title in his own copy of the score, which, as Lawrence Gilman tells us in his *Edward MacDowell: A Study*, reads, "First Symphonic Poem (a. 'Hamlet'; b. 'Ophelia')." This new title shows that the two works are to be considered as a unit, complementing each other in their contents. Their thematic material is in fact identical to a certain extent, though developed differently in the two sections.

All together twenty-six performances of MacDowell's works are recorded in the Boston programs from 1889 to 1945. But of these only three performances have occurred in the last twenty years. This manifest neglect of an artist, generally considered the most outstanding American composer of the late nineteenth century, can be partially explained by the current interest in the activities of the young newcomers. Nevertheless, this shortcoming should be corrected.

With Foote, Loeffler, Hadley, Chadwick, and MacDowell, the leading American composers from about 1880 to 1930 have withdrawn from active participation in the musical scene of America. With the exception of Loeffler, whose music still commands attention, the others will be remembered through only a small selection of their most characteristic and accomplished works, performed on special occasions. It must be remembered, however, that in the case of MacDowell symphonic music represents only a secondary part of his artistic output; he was mainly a composer of piano music.

Our survey turns now to the intermediate generation, younger than the group just mentioned but older than the modernists at present claiming public attention. This intermediate group, as far as its relations to the Boston Symphony Orchestra are concerned, is led by Henry F. Gilbert, Daniel Gregory Mason, David Stanley Smith, Edward B. Hill, Frederick S. Converse, John Alden Carpenter, Charles T. Griffes, Emerson Whithorne, Deems Taylor, and Louis Gruenberg. Their creative activity started about 1900 and reaches into the forties. A characteristic trait of some of them is the stress laid on Americanism, in many cases an Americanism of a peculiar brand—descriptive of American scenery and ways of life, attainments of the machine age, etc.— that was superseded by a new phase of Americanism, based on folklore, which has dominated the last fifteen years.

The oldest of the group is Henry F. Gilbert (1868–1928). A

distinct individual, whose works are not conveniently considered with other productions of the group, he will be discussed later. Of the other members of the intermediate generation, those representing the classical symphonic German style may first be singled out for closer inspection.

Daniel Gregory Mason—a member of a family notable in American music, a pupil of Paine at Harvard, later himself professor of music at Columbia University—is listed a single time in Koussevitzky's programs with his Symphony in C minor, Opus 11, on March 16, 1928. This work, the second version of a much older symphony that had been played in Philadelphia, Detroit, and New York, made a second round of the major American concert halls, but it has in late years disappeared from programs, sharing the fate of almost all symphonies thus far written in America. In his subsequent works Mason has taken his place with the conservative wing of recent American music, trusting more to Brahms as a guiding star than to Stravinsky. He is not in quest of sensational modernism but of solid structural art, clearly profiled melody, and logical development of his thematic material. Fantastic programmatic ideas, jazz, and noisy Americanism are absent from his distinguished work, which one might call a legitimate successor to Arthur Foote's music, with its characteristic New England reticence.

David Stanley Smith, for many years the head of the Yale University School of Music, has been a prolific composer in the fields of chamber, choral, and symphonic music. In the January 1942 issue of the *Musical Quarterly*, B. C. Tuthill has written an informative appraisal of the art of this too-little-known American composer. What is called modernism is not in any respect the aim of Smith's art. One may perhaps most aptly call it a continuation of the Brahms manner, plus a certain rejuvenation resulting from the technical innovations of the twentieth century. Never sensational, the art of D. S. Smith is, nonetheless, rich in musical values, solid in substance, warm in sentiment. The Boston Symphony Orchestra has performed four of his works. Monteux conducted in 1921 and 1923 Smith's "Poem of Youth," Opus 47, and "Fête Galante," Opus 48, for flute and orchestra, with Georges Laurent as soloist. Koussevitzky added on April 12, 1935, the "Epic Poem," Opus 55, conducted by the composer. The title does not refer to a particular literary epic poem, but is derived from the epic quality of the music, which the composer sees "in the mystical introduction, the faster music that follows, with its graceful beginning but martial and threatening development section, and the solemn music at the end." The last work of Smith heard in Boston, at this writing, was his Symphony No. 4, Opus 78, conducted for the first time by the composer on April 14, 1939. The four movements follow the traditional formal pattern of the classical symphony, not rigidly, but with certain deviations, in a modern sense. The music is rich in thematic material and thematic development, varied in character, ingenious in its polyphonic treatment, and plastic and expressive in its motives and melodies.

In his symphonies Edward Burlingame Hill (b. 1871), a Harvard professor of music, has features that parallel those of his colleagues Mason of Columbia and D. S. Smith of Yale. Their tendencies are about alike, their style similar. Their aim is not sensation or provocative novelty but substantial, sound musical contents; logical structure; and a quiet, inherent Americanism that contrasts with the noisy, pretentious Americanism in vogue for some time. Yet Hill's art, spanning four decades, has gone through at least three phases and appears to be less static than the art of Mason and Smith. From the start, Hill's symphonic music has had closest relation with the Boston Symphony Orchestra. His numerous works have been written for the Orchestra, performed by it, and inspired and assisted in their progress by his life-time proximity with this magnificent group of musicians. Hill's three phases are French impressionism, pure, non-descriptive symphonic music, and the modern constructivism of a neoclassic type.

When Koussevitzky commenced his activities in Boston, Hill had already arrived at his second phase, after taking leave of impressionism in one of his most distinguished scores, "Lilacs." Inspired by Amy Lowell's beautiful and gentle poem of the same title, Hill wrote a delicate, colorful, refined score. A romantic ecstasy animates the piece. Portraying "Heart leaves of lilac all over New England," its sensitive tones suggest the manifold tints of the lilac clusters, and the piece closes with an enraptured outburst of affection for the composer's native region. The lessons learned from French impressionism are here applied in a regional spirit; and Hill's "Lilacs" becomes truly American music because the emotion underlying it is truly American. One does not hear the loudly shouting voice of robust young America, but tones of a poet who speaks gently, sincerely, and touches those with a heart for New England's beauty. "Lilacs" was performed four times by Koussevitzky: in 1927, 1930, 1935, and 1942.

On March 30, 1928, Koussevitzky brought out for the first time Hill's latest score, First Symphony, Opus 34. Though one cannot call this symphony a work of militant Americanism or a confession of radical modernism, it still is a masterpiece. Its well-balanced and happily proportioned form, its genuine lyricism, plastic and melodious themes, its interesting symphonic development, its generally agreeable, optimistic mood, and its finish and polish of diction are a far cry from the problematic experimentalism, overheated imagination, roughness and loudness of many recent American works. It is easy, as often happens, to look down on a work of this type as being reactionary, not up-to-date, yet it is very hard to reproduce its balance and finished blend of all factors. This symphony, like Hill's "Lilacs," was heard four times, in 1928, 1929, 1934, and 1943.

Hill's Second Symphony in C major had its first hearing on February 27, 1931. In his brief explanatory notes in the program book, the composer was evidently desirous of making clear his position in the new American music. He disclaimed any inclination towards descriptive music and "literary quotations." He had come to believe that "music has enough intrinsic problems of its own without adding those of other arts." This confession of faith, also applicable to the First Symphony of 1928, meant a change of style. In his earlier works Hill was not at all averse to the descriptive tendencies, the pictorial charms, and the literary associations of French impressionistic music, as is evident by the precise descriptive titles of his earlier symphonic poems, and of "Stevensoniana" and "Lilacs." But Hill has not only separated himself from his first love, impressionism; he has also refused to be a partisan of the new boisterous radicalism in music, and he acknowledges candidly that he "had not had sufficient experience to experiment." He comes to the conclusion that the traditional forms offer enough opportunities for him to exercise his inventive, expressive, and constructive powers. But whoever expects after this declaration of faith to hear an orthodox, somewhat old-fashioned symphony will be disappointed, and, one might add, agreeably so. He will hear straightforward, unproblematic, yet colorful, carefully balanced, amiable, and refined music; rich in interesting detail as regards melodic material, harmony, lyric expressiveness, and polyphonic elaboration. In short, refined taste and something serene and amiable gives Hill's later works a unique and distinctive position in recent American music, which generally lacks just these qualities no matter how else it may excel.

Hill's Third Symphony, Opus 41, written in 1936, was brought out by Koussevitzky for the first time on December 3, 1937. Written in the idyllic, bright, and peaceful key of G major, the score offers no surprises, presents no new problems. The composer's genial mood and his friendly intercourse with the instruments of the orchestra, the easy and gentle flow of the music, and the finish and elegance of its form assert themselves as positive, valuable factors. The character of the first movement is aptly indicated in its designation, "Allegro grazioso ma con brio." Does one ever meet a real and sincere *grazioso* in the scores of our young modernists? Hill's grazioso is not parodistic as in current ballet music, but the genuine article, sufficiently tempered *con brio* to prevent an excess of mildness. The plentiful, exciting, and brilliant percussion group of the Orchestra did its part to realize the Allegro energico of the finale.

Another work was added to the long list of Hill's compositions heard in Boston when Koussevitzky introduced Hill's new Violin Concerto, Opus 38, on November 11, 1938. The score reveals no new traits in the well-defined and familiar features of Hill's art. It was brilliantly played by Ruth Posselt, certainly one of the most accomplished women violinists to be found in any country.*

In his third phase Hill also paid due tribute to the prevailing trend for the orchestral concerto, the concertino, and the sinfonietta, a useful and practical procedure for economizing time and labor. Two concertinos or sinfoniettas are about the equivalent of one full-grown symphony; and in fortunate consequence these smaller forms have increased opportunity for public performance. A new Concertino for Piano and Orchestra, Opus 36, had its first performance on April 25, 1932, and was repeated on March 9, 1933. At both occasions Jesús María Sanromá, pianist to the Orchestra, was the soloist. It should be noted that the services rendered by this excellent artist to the cause of a new piano music are very considerable. In the course of years he has played the solo part in Ernst Toch's Concerto, Bloch's Concerto grosso, Stravinsky's Capriccio, Ravel's Concerto, Mario Pilati's Suite, and Constant Lambert's "The Rio Grande." He has also been soloist in Honegger's Concertino and Piston's Concertino, as well as in Hill's Concertino. The number of concertinos in this list is illustrative of the recent trend, mentioned above, toward conciseness and brevity, coupled with thematic variety. Seventy-five years earlier Liszt wrote concertos in one movement, with scanty thematic material, varied in rhythm and tempo to serve the composition's four sections. This monothematic principle, later adopted by César Franck as *principe cyclique,* has not been taken over by the modern concertino writers. Hill, in his notes for the program book, expressly disavows any use of the "cyclical method," although he concedes a "family resemblance between the themes of the different sections." Other features common to the modern concertinos are the absence of showy virtuosity

---

* After years of extended concert tours all over Europe and America, Ruth Posselt has at last settled down more permanently in Boston as the wife of concertmaster Richard Burgin. Her extraordinary capacities have been revealed not only in her mastery of the entire violinistic repertory but also in her devotion to the task of learning by heart and performing in public a number of modern American concertos written expressly for her by Hill, Piston, Dukelsky, and Barber.

(which is replaced by a certain intentional sobriety of expression, best explained by the French word *sec*), and a terse, slender structure, devoid of ornamental design.

In 1932 at Koussevitzky's suggestion, Hill wrote a new shorter symphonic work, Sinfonietta in One Movement, Opus 37, which had its first performance on March 10, 1933. This symphony in miniature compresses three movements into the space of one. Again the composer stresses the absence of a "descriptive background."

Hill's Sinfonietta, Opus 40a, had its first performances not in Boston but during a tour of the Boston Orchestra in Brooklyn and New York, on April 3 and 4, 1936. This sinfonietta is a version for string orchestra of Hill's String Quartet, Opus 40, performed by the Chardon Quartet in January 1936 at Cambridge. The orchestral transcription was due to a suggestion of Koussevitzky. The four movements of this amiable work raise no problems, open no vistas to unknown regions. Yet they satisfy the musical mind with their finely balanced form, interesting thematic elaboration, lyric charm, and adequate and agreeable sound effect. At the conclusion of the Harvard Tercentenary Celebration in September 1936 this composition was heard twice on the same day; at noon the complete string quartet version was played, and at night part of the sinfonietta.

After his Concertino of 1932 and his two sinfoniettas of 1933 and 1936, Hill wrote a new Concertino for String Orchestra, Opus 46, brought out for the first time by Koussevitzky on April 19, 1940. It might just as well have been called a sinfonietta, as its first movement is written in an abbreviated sonata form, and its Andante applies the ternary song form with contrasting intermezzo currently used in many sonatas and symphonies. Only the finale stresses the concerto grosso idea, being built upon one theme only; and opposing the so-called "concertino"— here a solo string quartet—to the "concerto grosso," the "tutti" of the string orchestra.

Edward B. Hill was one of the two American composers honored by Koussevitzky with a commission for the jubilee season of the Orchestra, 1930–1931. His contribution was an Ode

for Chorus based on a poem that Robert Hillyer had written
expressly for the occasion. The performance took place on October 17, 1930. The poet himself read his Ode. Its four six-line
stanzas, three couples of rhyme in each, are printed in the program book. This poem's basic idea is the music of the spheres:

> And Earth's reverberant echoes climb
> To sweet accord with her companion stars.

The composer did not fail to utilize in his score the instrumental hints of the poem.* The instruments of the Orchestra
are called upon to make their characteristic contribution to
the celestial music of the universe: the "windy flute of pastoral
themes"; the harp to "remember leafy light, that danced above
our younger days"; the violins of graver phrase to "follow love
with voices down the night"; and the "bannered horn of golden
doom" and the trumpets to "mildly hail the trumpets calling
clear from farther shores"—perhaps an allusion to the day of
resurrection. But, strangely, the poem fails to assign some appropriate cosmic duty to the voices of the chorus. The choral
part was confided to the Harvard Glee Club and the Radcliffe
Choral Society, which have through Koussevitzky's twenty-two
years become closely allied with the Boston Symphony Orchestra in works demanding a large chorus. Professor Archibald T.
Davison and Professor G. Wallace Woodworth expertly trained
these groups for their part in Hill's Ode.

Hill's latest work is "Music for English Horn and Orchestra,"
Opus 50, performed for the first time by Koussevitzky on March
2, 1945. English horn players will be grateful for this addition
to their scanty literature, all the more so as the work allows
the player to show the resources of his instrument to best advantage. This piece is also enjoyable to the listener—beautiful
music with a romantic touch, written so masterfully that it over-
comes all problematic impediments. Mr. Louis Speyer, the
English horn soloist of the Orchestra, gave an exceptionally fine
rendering of this composition.

---

* Handel in his "Ode on St. Cecilia's Day" and "Alexander's Feast"
—both to Dryden's verses—treated a similar idea.

CHAPTER 4

SECOND PHASE OF AMERICAN
SYMPHONIC WRITING

A new type of American symphonic writing is found in the works of Thompson, Hanson, Hadley, Hill, Mason, Smith. They all adhere, at least in a part of their production, to the classical and romantic type of the German symphony. Yet there is a difference between their symphonies and those of the still older American masters, notably Paine and Chadwick. The latter stem from Beethoven, Schumann, Schubert, whereas the younger group is in addition influenced by Brahms, Tchaikovsky, Rimsky-Korsakoff, César Franck, Sibelius, Wagner.

Randall Thompson's music reached Boston's Symphony Hall for the first time on April 13, 1934, when Koussevitzky conducted his Symphony No. 2. Years earlier Thompson had established his reputation as an exceptionally well-equipped American composer of moderately modern tendency. Educated at Harvard, a pupil of Ernest Bloch, and winner of the American Prix de Rome, he entered a professional career as lecturer, teacher of composition, and choral conductor at various colleges and universities. He was director of the Curtis Institute in Philadelphia, 1939–1941, and since 1941 has been head of the department of music at the University of Virginia.

In his orchestral works one can observe the change of taste and style around 1930 that a number of cases have already illustrated. Thompson commenced with a symphonic poem, "The Piper at the Gates of Dawn" (performed at Sanders Theatre, Cambridge, in 1929 by the Boston Symphony Orchestra); paid his tribute to the novelty of the day in "A Jazz Poem" for pianoforte and orchestra; and then turned to symphonic music devoid of fanciful titles. Of his second symphony he wrote in the program book, "It is based on no programme, either literary or spiritual. It is not cyclical. I wanted to write four contrasting

movements, separate and distinct, which together should convey
a sense of balance and completeness." Thompson's symphonic
style is akin to Hill's in that it maintains the symphonic classical
tradition, is not intent on a dazzling display of radical modernism, but presents music of high artistic quality, melodic distinction and charm, and rhythmical interest and vitality. The advocates of sensational modernism will not likely be satisfied with
this type of music. Yet, though not revolutionary in spirit, it has
an evolutionary value. Thompson's symphonic style is by no
means old-fashioned. It stresses a friendly outlook on the world;
takes delight in amiable, agreeable expression; and with quiet
and quaint humor, it maintains that ferocious, aggressive, cyni-
cal, burlesque, passionate and angry outcries are not the only
legitimate factors of modern music, and that gentler, more
civilized modes of expression also have a legitimate place in
art as well as in life. With all its self-imposed limitations, the
symphonic music of Thompson like that of Hill has in its
thematic material a decided American groundtone, akin to what
MacDowell's piano music sometimes exhales; for instance, in the
"Woodland Sketches," where certain melodic turns and accents
strongly suggest the New England atmosphere.

A second outstanding work by Randall Thompson was the
"Alleluia" for chorus, written by him for the opening of Koussevitzky's Berkshire Music Center in the summer of 1940. This
piece, for chorus a cappella, is one of the most accomplished
works of its kind and establishes Thompson as a real master of
choral writing in the classical sense. Inspired by Handel, the
greatest master of choral art, this "Alleluia" with its plastic lines
of melody, its surging waves of sound, its colorful effect, is,
nevertheless, a modern work of art, representing a renaissance
of the classic vocal art. It was sung by the Berkshire Music Center
Chorus, conducted by G. Wallace Woodworth.

Under the title of "The Testament of Freedom," Randall
Thompson has set to music four passages from the writings of
Thomas Jefferson, for men's voices and orchestra. The first
Boston performance of this new work was conducted by Kous-
sevitzky on April 7, 1945. The composition was written for the

celebration of Jefferson's two hundredth anniversary, at the University of Virginia, founded by Jefferson. The first glance at the printed piano score reveals a rather unusual simplicity for a modern choral work. Homophonic declamation prevails; the chorus often sings in unison or in octaves, or the recitation progresses in rather plain chords. The orchestra is in the main content with establishing an effective background; it refrains almost entirely from involved and extended symphonic monologues; and in the few places where it is heard alone it provides a short bridge from one choral section to the next one. All this sounds well and is appropriate. Much is achieved by Thompson with few means—a sign of mastery. Yet one might question whether still more might not have been achieved with a more plentiful dose of imagination. The sublime thoughts of Jefferson, here sensibly but somewhat dryly expressed in music, can certainly stand a richer, bolder, musical interpretation. Of late the idea has been exploited of musically portraying the great figures of American history. Carpenter was, it seems, the first to glorify George Washington by choral recitation of famous passages from his writings. Several Lincoln portraits followed, notably Aaron Copland's interesting symphonic frame for stirring sections of the Gettysburg and other addresses. Randall Thompson continues the series with his choral Jefferson apology. One might next reasonably expect Wilson's Fourteen Points, treated for chorus or double chorus with orchestra, and Roosevelt's and Churchill's Atlantic Charter as a theme for a symphony with chorus. Possibly there is danger in a new genre of routine taking over the great names of the country's history, for political wisdom and great humanitarian ideas as a rule are not grateful texts for musical treatment.

Howard Hanson, now a well-known figure in American music, made his first appearance in Boston with a major work on April 5, 1929, when his First Symphony, Opus 21, was performed. Since 1924 director of the richly endowed Eastman School of Music in Rochester, New York, Hanson has patronized American music systematically and successfully by his annual festivals of American music. Of Swedish descent, he has Nordic affiliations that can be traced in many of his works. His First Symphony bears the epithet "Nordic." The strength of this Scandinavian trend is evident in the fact that the Nordic Symphony was written in the South—at Rome, where Hanson spent three years. He went there as winner of the recently established American Prix de Rome in 1921. Several other Nordic works came into existence in Rome, "North and West," and "The Lament for Beowulf." It is hardly surprising that Hanson's First Symphony, with its pronounced Nordic—more Swedish than Norwegian—background, does not abound in Americanisms or in modernistic traits. Its sound musical value must have impressed Koussevitzky considerably, however, otherwise he would probably not have commissioned Hanson to write a new symphonic work expressly for the jubilee season. Hanson and E. B. Hill were the two American composers thus honored by Koussevitzky.

Hanson's Second Symphony, written for the fiftieth anniversary season and performed by Koussevitzky for the first time on November 28, 1930, carries the subtitle, "Romantic." This title is a confession of faith, like the title "Nordic" of the First Symphony. Contrary to the anti-romantic trend of the present epoch, Hanson has expressed his belief in the continued vitality of the romantic ideals. "Romanticism," he has written, "will find in this country rich soil for a new, young, and vigorous growth." He thus disclaims any reactionary, academic tendencies and claims a legitimate place for romanticism in new American music. His aim in this symphony was "to create a work young in spirit, romantic in temperament, and simple and direct in expression." That he found weighty support in this goal has been shown by the considerable number of performances of this symphony in America as well as in London, Paris, Berlin, Amsterdam, and elsewhere. At Boston Symphony concerts this Romantic Symphony has been played four times: once in 1931 and 1939 and twice in 1941—a rare distinction for a modern American symphony.

Hanson's Third Symphony was written in 1936–1937 by request of the Columbia Broadcasting System, then sponsoring a series of new American orchestral works. It was heard twice over the air before its first concert performance in Boston, conducted by the composer on November 3, 1939. Koussevitzky later performed it twice, on March 21, 1940, and March 9, 1945. Unlike Hanson's two earlier symphonies, it has no special title. Yet it is not difficult to discover that like the Nordic Symphony it, too, is animated by the spirit of the North; so much so that after the performance in 1945 the critic of the Boston *Globe,* Cyrus Durgin, called it "Sibelius," which one might conclude to mean a sort of synthesis of the Nordic and Romantic symphonies. Though a relationship to Sibelius can easily be perceived in Hanson's score, so earnest and weighty a work cannot be disposed of simply with a label suggesting an undue imitation of the great Finnish master. A symphony may well show the influence of another, greater master and yet be impressive and of substantial value. In the words of the composer, found in the Boston Symphony program book, the new symphony "pays tribute to the epic qualities of those [Swedish] pioneers" in America, on the Delaware and in the West. The first movement, Andante lamentando, expresses the state of mind of those pioneers by its "rugged and turbulent character, alternating with a religious mysticism." The quiet and peaceful slow movement suggests well-earned rest after the toilsome labor of the day. Merriment is the signature of the Scherzo, a rhythmically vigorous and brilliant piece that sticks in the memory of the listener and has individuality in spite of a likeness to certain Sibelius pieces. The powerfully built finale has monumental traits as it moves from melancholy brooding to the consolation of a chorale and thence to a decidedly optimistic close of grateful and joyful confidence. One might agree with N.S. in his review in the *New York Times* (March 1945) that this symphony "after its first movement, begins to pall with its constant unrelieved richness of scoring," and yet not accept his impression that the building up of mighty climaxes leads nowhere in particular. Even if the explosions à la Wagner and Tchaikovsky do not come off with an equal brilliance, the constructive force of the symphony is considerable.

In an interview published in the Boston program book of November 3, 1939, Hanson expounded his views of Americanism in music. He does not favor "conscious nationalism," that is, the obligation to use "folk-tunes or Indian melodies." The only true Americanism for him "creeps in when the composer isn't looking." The American composer should "express himself, not his country, in music," and if he is a genuine American, his music will have American flavor, even without any external national features. Actually this simple theory of unconscious and unintentional Americanism may satisfy a musician of Hanson's peculiar mentality and yet be vigorously opposed by such artists as Gilbert, Gershwin, and Harris.

Hanson's Fourth Symphony had its first performance on December 3, 1943, in a concert of the Boston Symphony Orchestra, conducted by the composer. One of the noblest works ever written in America, this symphony does not merely play with structural problems—a technical, intellectual practice that may be highly ingenious and interesting and yet degrade the psychic, emotional factor to relative unimportance. On the contrary, Hanson's symphony is primarily concerned with expressive values; these emotional, personal outbursts, however, are subject to a by no means slight structural art.

As a tribute to his father, Hanson wrote a Requiem Mass for orchestra only, its four movements corresponding to the Kyrie, Requiescat, Dies irae, and Lux aeterna of the Mass. Yet this is not merely a solemn, ecclesiastic work of art. Opposing its religious emotions dealing with the mystery of death are the joys and sorrows, doubts and turmoil of human life. And the composition gains its peculiar individual character by this very mixture, this intertwining of the two fundamental conditions of the world of nature—life and death. Thus the first movement (Andante inquieto) states its Kyrie theme in a somber, prayerful mood, merging—like a reminiscence of happy, bygone days—into a scherzando episode. This gradually changes over into an appassionato, which, as a complement and counter-theme, introduces a solemn chorale, thus restoring the religious mood and convincingly and logically leading back the Kyrie theme. Both the Kyrie theme and the chorale recur in later movements in diverse transformations as basic thematic material.

The second movement, corresponding to the Requiescat, is a sustained largo based on a scale theme sung at first by the bassoon, to which other groups of instruments respond. The chorale reappears in the background. Only a few sinister and threatening accents are superimposed on this serious, subdued, and rather calm piece.

In violent contrast the Dies irae movement cries out its agony and fear in a bitter and fierce presto, a scherzo with a diabolic touch. Here the Kyrie theme dwindles into insignificance, giving way to still more agitated outbursts.

The Lux aeterna finale, largo pastorale, mixes calm, almost idyllic, expression with violent interjections in dramatic discourse. The chorale and the Kyrie are used impressively as the piece approaches its solemn and sublime close, in peaceful breadth. The Lux aeterna shines forth miraculously, spreading consolation and peace. In addition to chorale and Kyrie theme a number of salient and characteristic shorter motives tie the four movements together, into a closely interwoven, organic unit.

Arthur Shepherd's name occurs only twice in the Boston programs: on April 15, 1921, when Monteux conducted his Fantasy for Piano and Orchestra, with Heinrich Gebhard as soloist, and on November 1, 1942, when Shepherd conducted his Symphony No. 2. Born in Idaho in 1880, Shepherd spent many years in Boston as a pupil of Chadwick, Goetschius, and Elson at the New England Conservatory, later as a teacher at the same conservatory, and for a short time as conductor of the Cecilia Society Chorus. In later years Shepherd's activities have centered in Cleveland, where he has been a music critic, assistant conductor of the Cleveland Orchestra, and director of the music department of Western Reserve University. Though the list of his compositions includes numerous orchestral and choral works as well as much chamber music, his music has been heard so rarely in Boston and New York that it is hardly possible to get an adequate estimate of his art.

The name of Gardner Read occurred for the first time on a Boston Symphony program when Koussevitzky conducted his

Suite for String Orchestra, Opus 33a, on December 30, 1938. This young composer from Illinois (b. 1913), a pupil of the Eastman School of Music in Rochester, was the winner of the first prize in a competition sponsored by the New York Philharmonic–Symphony Society in 1936. The award honored his first symphony, which he had written as a fellow of the MacDowell Colony at Peterborough, New Hampshire. The list of his orchestral and chamber-music compositions is quite extensive. The suite performed at Boston is an arrangement for string orchestra of a string quartet, consisting of a Prelude, Scherzetto, Sarabande, and Rondo. The prelude, *adagio e semplice,* is the weightiest part of the suite. It is followed by a brief scherzo, a meditative saraband, *andante sostenuto,* and a rondo finale, *allegretto, quasi burlesca.* The easy flowing, melodious, and in parts spirited work has a popular appeal and has deservedly been heard a number of times in various cities.

Read conducted his Second Symphony, Opus 45, at its first performance on November 26, 1943. The titles of the three movements suggest that the composer was intent on unorthodox procedures. The first movement, Presto assai e molto feroce, proposes a kind of violent and relentless activity generally reserved for a finale. The finale, naturally, must still outdo the first movement, and therefore embarks on an Allegro frenetico, preceded and followed by a Largamente section. Between these two agitated pieces an Adagio e molto mesto is expanded in a somber and profoundly sad mood. A dramatic, passionate work with tragic accents, dynamic effects, and strange sonorities, it is very different in character from the much lighter, almost popular, earlier suite.

CHAPTER 5

FRENCH IMPRESSIONISM AND EXOTICISM
IN AMERICAN MUSIC

The influence exerted by the art of Debussy and Ravel on American composers commenced rather slowly after 1900. Before that date American musicians usually went to Germany to finish their professional education, Vienna, Berlin, Leipzig, and Munich being especially favored. The contrapuntal training given by the famous Munich teacher Joseph Rheinberger appeared indispensable to most American students seriously interested in composition. After Rheinberger's death, in 1901, Munich lost much of its attraction. American students of composition began to turn to Paris, where great teachers like Widor, d'Indy, and Koechlin had much to offer them, and after the first World War Paris became the favorite choice of American students. The music school in the castle of Fontainebleau, founded especially for the Americans, and Nadia Boulanger became the great attractions and remained so until about 1935.

Most American composers born between 1880 and 1900 have been more or less fascinated by the subtle refinement of the French impressionistic masters. Of those heard in Boston, Loeffler, E. B. Hill, Deems Taylor, Carpenter, and Converse have clearly reflected the impressionistic methods in their productions —but only in a part of them. Their work will be considered more in detail in the discussions of classical symphony and illustrative program music. A few others, like Griffes, George Foote, Steinert, Harl McDonald, and Mabel Daniels, whose compositions are mainly impressionistic in character, find their proper place here, as well as those exploiting exotic music, like Eichheim, Hadley, Fairchild, and Schelling.

Charles T. Griffes is now considered one of America's most promising and gifted musicians. When he died in 1920, at the age of thirty-six, his musical productions had not yet reached full maturity. Yet he left a small number of works that will be sure of an honored place in the history of American music. Among these the orchestral composition "The Pleasure Dome of Kubla Khan" has won special acclaim. This score had its first performance by Pierre Monteux and the Boston Symphony Orchestra in 1919; was repeated in 1920; and Koussevitzky conducted it on April 24, 1931. The piece was inspired, of course, by Coleridge's famous poem "Kubla Khan." Griffes needed fantastic scenery of some sort to stimulate his inventive and creative powers, for his music gained shape and color best when it was suggested by a series of imaginary pictures. Thus various sections of the score refer to the sacred river Alph, running "through caverns measureless to man down to a sunless sea," then to the palace "with walls and towers girdled round," the "gardens bright with sinuous rills," and the ancient forests "enfolding sunny spots of greenery." One hears the addition that the composer made to the description of the poet—"sounds of dancing and revelry" rising to a rapturous outburst and suddenly disappearing, when in the coda the sacred river continues its calm, mysterious course to the "caves of ice."

This is descriptive program music, somewhat in the manner of Smetana's "Vltava" ("The Moldau") with its picturesque, changing scenery; but Griffes brings to it the sensitive, colorful technique of modern French impressionism. His "Pleasure Dome" is in fact one of the most impressive compositions of its type, in a class with Respighi's "Le Fontane di Roma" and a few other select pieces. Griffes died too early to be much affected by the new anti-romantic trend of "absolute" music, or neo-classicism, or the rising tide of Americanism.

A smaller work of Griffes was performed at Symphony Hall during the following season, on January 15, 1932, at a concert conducted by Chalmers Clifton. This "Poem" for flute and orchestra is a valuable addition to the scanty concert literature for the flute. It gave the soloist, Georges Laurent * a welcome and

* Since 1918 Mr. Laurent, a *premier prix* of the Paris Conservatory, has been first flutist of the Boston Symphony Orchestra. He is also the founder of the Boston Flute Players Club, an organization that for more than twenty years has devoted its efforts mainly to new or rarely heard chamber music.

rare opportunity to show his accomplished art to best advantage.

George Foote (b. 1886) received his musical education partly at Harvard and in Boston, partly in Paris and Berlin. Two of his refined and carefully elaborated orchestral scores have been performed by Koussevitzky: "Variations on a Pious Theme," on February 11, 1935, repeated a few days later at Sanders Theatre, Cambridge, and the suite "In Praise of Winter" on January 5, 1940. Both works, limited to the generally accepted procedures of twentieth-century music, are without any experimental tendencies, any excursions into novel, unexplored regions. In this conservative, though not by any means reactionary, tendency, George Foote is a companion of composers like E. B. Hill and Randall Thompson. The four impressionistic pieces entitled "In Praise of Winter" do not aim at describing any winter sport activities or any particularly impressive snow scenery, but are intended to convey, in the words of the composer, "something of the atmosphere of what Thomas Wolfe called the beautiful frozen north."

Alexander Lang Steinert, born in Boston, a pupil of Loeffler, a graduate of the Harvard Music Department in the class of 1922, subsequently became one of the Americans who made their homes in Paris and returned to America only as temporary guests. He studied with Koechlin and Vincent d'Indy, was admitted to Gedalge's class in fugue at the Conservatory, and profited from Ravel's critical reviews of his compositions. One need not be surprised, therefore, that his music sounds more Parisian than American. An accomplished pianist, Steinert played the important piano part in Koussevitzky's performances of Scriabin's "Prometheus," in the spring of 1925. On October 15, 1926, Koussevitzky performed Steinert's poem for orchestra, "Southern Night." In 1927 Steinert was awarded the American Prix de Rome. Long residence in Rome, as well as in Paris, evidently did more toward developing his already marked Latin tendencies than his American affiliations. In Rome the "Leggenda Sinfonica" came into existence, and Koussevitzky performed it for the first time in America on March 13, 1931. The score is inscribed "To the Boston Symphony Orchestra on its Fiftieth Anniversary." A few months earlier it had been played for the very first time at the Augusteo in Rome, conducted by Howard Hanson, like Steinert a recipient of the Prix de Rome.

Steinert last appeared with the Orchestra on February 8, 1935, when he played the solo part of his "Concerto Sinfonico" for piano and orchestra. Written in one extended continuous movement, the piece nevertheless gives the impression of the traditional three movements, making use of the same thematic material throughout. In the symphonic structure and the elaboration of thematic development, the composer's considerable skill and maturity are evident. In its entire attitude the concerto is more akin to the French style of 1930 than to the contemporary endeavors for a specifically American style.

Harl McDonald, at present manager of the Philadelphia Orchestra and choral conductor at the University of Pennsylvania, a well-known composer, is represented in Koussevitzky's programs by "San Juan Capistrano," two nocturnes for orchestra, heard for the first time on October 30, 1939. This score is impressionistic music; "The Mission" paints with delicate and suggestive sonorities the convent atmosphere at the old Mexican border town of Capistrano. This charming peaceful evening scene with ecclesiastic touch is followed in effective contrast by a lively dance scene in Spanish style, "Fiesta," in which the ever popular Spanish-Colonial Jota and a danza-dueto in Habanera tempo are brought to an impressive climax.

The name of Mabel Daniels occurs twice on the Boston programs; the first time on April 15, 1932, when Koussevitzky and the Cecilia Society Chorus performed her "Exultate Deo" for mixed chorus and orchestra, a composition still well liked and found on numerous programs in various cities. The first public performance, on April 5, 1931, by the Handel and Haydn Society, conducted by Thompson Stone, must have made a good impression, for Koussevitzky repeated it a year later. This psalm motet had been composed expressly for the fiftieth anniversary of Radcliffe College and was heard for the first time in a private performance conducted by G. Wallace Woodworth in May 1929. Miss Daniels, a graduate of Radcliffe College, later a student of composition with Chadwick and with Ludwig Thuille in Munich, is one of the few American women who have won distinction as composers. She has specialized in choral music and for many years has been considerably successful in this field.

For the second time Koussevitzky conducted one of her works when her prelude for small orchestra "Deep Forest" was heard in a new arrangement for a larger orchestra on April 16, 1937. The title "Deep Forest" may have suggested itself because the composition was written at the MacDowell colony in the forests of New Hampshire. The composer modestly writes that "this little piece makes no pretense at being other than a simple prelude, frankly impressionistic in style." Yet this simple prelude has charms and refinements of sound and has been heard with pleasure on many occasions.

Closely allied with the impressionists is a group of American composers preoccupied with oriental and exotic themes. The earliest one in this group is Henry Eichheim, for many years a member of the Boston Symphony Orchestra in the first violin section before he was lured to the Far East, where he spent years of travel and study. His "Chinese Legend," performed in Koussevitzky's first season, has already been mentioned. Orientalism that is nearly undiluted pervades Henry Eichheim's symphonic poems "Java" and "Burma," heard on November 15, 1929, under the composer's direction. "Java" employs some genuine Malay tunes and mixes western orchestral instruments with a set of genuine bells and percussion instruments of the Javanese gamelan orchestra, brought to America by Eichheim. The "Burma" music was originally written for an oriental play by Irene Lewisohn, produced in New York in 1926, and later expanded into an orchestral concert piece. Authentic Burmese dances, melodies, and instruments imparted an exotic charm to this play, on which H. T. Parker, critic of the *Boston Evening Transcript*, wrote an interesting report, reprinted in the Boston program book. In addition, the composer's own statements in the program help to explain the nature of his music. Part I "establishes the mood of twilight on the platform of the Shwe Dagon in Rangoon, during which peasants, priests . . . water-carriers, children playing their games . . . and many other types of devout Burmese gather at the base of this wonderful pagoda, with its myriad shrines and small shops. The strange clangor of dissonant bells and gongs lingers on the memory as night closes this picture." Part II is concerned with the "Pwé," a ceremonial Burmese entertainment, consisting of three dances: "The Prince and the Princess"; "Grotesquerie," the clownish dance of the Councillors; and the "Dance of Four Maids of Honor."

Eichheim's music was performed in a Boston Symphony Orchestra concert for the last time on November 23, 1934, when he conducted his symphonic poem "Bali." This score is a companion piece to "Java." Here some original Balinese melodies serve as thematic material. A considerable part is given over to the percussion instruments—drums, bells of many varieties, and other strange Javanese instruments of the gamelan being added to the conventional percussion group of the western orchestra. "Bali," the composer explains in the Boston program book, "is a series of variations within variations, formed on Balinese music which I heard in a temple court at Deupassar."

The group of exotic pieces by American composers includes Blair Fairchild's "Chants Nègres," performed by Koussevitzky on December 6, 1929. Fairchild, a graduate of Harvard in the class of 1899, a pupil of Paine and Spalding at Harvard, spent most of his later life in Europe, partly engaged in business, partly in the diplomatic service of the United States. In between he continued his musical studies in Florence and Paris. Finally he settled permanently in Paris, as a member of the American artists' colony. The list of his compositions in the Boston program book shows his interests in the Orient, mainly Persian and Hebrew, and his preference for Biblical titles. One may therefore assume that the "Chants Nègres" refers to African rather than American Negroes. But as the program contains scant notes on the composition and as the score is not immediately available here, more details on Fairchild's composition cannot be given.

Werner Josten makes his first appearance on a Boston program on April 19, 1929. Born and educated in Germany, he came to America in 1923 as instructor in the music department of Smith College, Northampton, Massachusetts. He has written

much choral music, besides some symphonic works. Of his Concerto Sacro for string orchestra and piano, Koussevitzky performed two movements. The conception of this work stems
from the deep impression made on the composer by Matthias
Grünewald's famous triptych painting for the Isenheim Altar at
Colmar in Alsace. It is a strange coincidence that about ten years
later Paul Hindemith took the idea for his opera *Mathis der
Maler* from the same painting. In passing, it is interesting to note
that at its first performance, in New York, on March 27, 1929,
Josten's Concerto Sacro had as companions on the program
Vaughan Williams' Concerto Academico and Bloch's Concerto
Grosso—a triptychon of concertos.

In the next season on October 25, 1929, Koussevitzky presented
a new score by Josten, the symphonic poem "Jungle." Coming so
soon after the performance of the Concerto Sacro, this second
work seems to indicate that Koussevitzky was favorably impressed
by the concerto. "Jungle" was also inspired by a painting—Henri
Rousseau's "Forêt exotique." As the composer informs us in the
program book, "the music tries to portray the emotions and sensations which assail a white man entering the jungle, with its
lures, terrors, primitive love and ferocious death." The unusually
large orchestra demanded to illustrate the mysterious sounds
and savage noises of this jungle includes an instrument called
"lion's roar," which must have been made especially for this
occasion. Although the composer states that "with the exception
of a Voodoo rhythmic motive, no native melodies or themes are
used," the composition belongs to the class of exotic pieces of
which a piece discussed below, "Morocco" by Ernest Schelling, is
a remarkable example.

The third and last work of Josten played by the Boston
Symphony Orchestra was his Symphony in F, conducted by the
composer on November 13, 1936. All three movements are based
on the same theme, composed of two different motives, one
ascending, one descending. This method of economy in melodic
invention invites a composer's ingenuity in devising a variety of
effects with identical thematic material, but it has its dangers
unless managed with extraordinary art, as the listener easily gets

tired of a threatening monotony. This danger Josten's symphony has not always sufficiently avoided.

Ernest Schelling, widely known as one of America's best pianists, was familiar to Boston's music lovers by his frequent recitals and as a soloist at the Symphony concerts. Four of his major compositions had already been heard at the Orchestra's performances prior to February 15, 1929, when he conducted his latest work, the symphonic poem "Morocco." One certainly cannot call this work American music; it makes use of tunes of the North African Berber tribes, which had greatly impressed the composer on a trip to Morocco. This piece expresses the exotic tendencies of the age, substituting for the dances and chants of the American Indians those of the Arab nomads. Schelling himself comments on his work in the Boston program book:

First there is the dance of the Ouled-Nails, with the strange, unforgettable yew-yew-yew cry of the women, which sweeps down over the assembly like a mist of sound.

Then comes the Lullaby, interrupted by the passing of the Caid and his followers. In this, as in their dances and songs, there is the constantly repeated figure, endless variations in the same tonality but with varying rhythm.

The third impression is of the Berber story-teller outside the walls of Fex at sunset, surrounded by hundreds of shrouded figures listening intently and fiercely to his constant repetition, always on one tone, of the glories of the past, and the fire-eater who works himself up into a frenzy.

Then the Baroud at Telout Kasbah, the mountain stronghold of El Glaoui, the great feudal lord of the Atlas. The working up of the war spirit among the tribes, again by insistent implacable rhythm.

The French and Russian literatures of music in the nineteenth and twentieth centuries abound in exotic pieces akin to Schelling's "Morocco."

CHAPTER 6

FIRST WAVE OF
AMERICANISM IN MUSIC

The first serious efforts at giving music an American local color
come from a few composers intent on utilizing for music the
discoveries in the field of North American Indian music at the
close of the nineteenth century. MacDowell's "Indian Suite" is
the most outstanding achievement in this line. It was written
about 1891–1892, and the main themes are based on genuine
Indian tunes. Koussevitzky performed "In War Time," one of the
suite's five movements, in April 1927. Before this time, between
1896 and 1917, the Orchestra had performed the entire suite
on eight occasions. Since 1927, however, this interesting work
has disappeared from the Orchestra's programs, and a revival
of the Indian Suite might be a rewarding experience. Charles
Wakefield Cadman is the leading specialist in music based on
Indian themes. His music, though not represented on the Boston
programs and at present almost totally neglected, should not be
lightly passed over in a detailed history of American music. A
remarkable and a more recent achievement in this class is Ferruccio Busoni's brilliant "Indianische Fantasie" for piano and
orchestra.

In the Boston programs one finds "Indian Dances" by Frederick Jacobi—a newcomer—making its first appearance on November 28, 1928. Koussevitzky conducted this work, which had just
been completed. Though little known in Boston, Jacobi's music
had in the early twenties been much performed in both America
and Europe, especially at several international festivals. A
native of San Francisco, Jacobi studied under Rubin Goldmark
in New York, Paul Juon in Berlin, and Ernest Bloch in Geneva.
On several journeys to New Mexico he had become greatly
interested in the music of the Indians and, in his own words,
"much impressed by the beauty and interest of their singing and

their dancing." The outcome of this is evident in a string quartet on Indian themes, played at the International Festival at Zurich in 1926, and in the orchestral suite heard in Boston. It comprises a Buffalo Dance, Butterfly Dance, War Dance, Rain Dance, and Corn Dance. In spite of the fascination of the Indian tunes and rhythms experienced by him, Jacobi believes that "there is no necessity for basing an American music on the music of the Indians or even the Negroes."

From about 1920 interest in Indian music flagged as Negro music was more and more exploited through jazz and Negro spirituals. In the nineties Antonín Dvořák had already called the attention of American musicians to the songs and dances of the Negroes, but for a long time he went unheeded by worthy successors in America.

The idea of national American music grew slowly. At the time of the first World War jazz made a big sensation and was exploited more as a business than an art. In the twenties a number of composers pursued the not very fertile but seductive idea of developing American music through illustrative program compositions treating stories and American scenery. This early wave of Americanism went out of fashion in the thirties and was replaced by another—dominant even now—when American folklore was discovered and utilized with superior judgment by a number of contemporary composers. All these phases are amply illustrated by dozens of compositions performed by Koussevitzky in Boston.

The first to form a clear idea of a national American art of music was Henry F. Gilbert. When his "Symphonic Piece" had its first performance on February 26, 1926, a new note was sounded at the Boston Symphony—a deliberate, outspoken Americanism, stronger than had so far been heard. The composer himself was quoted at length in Philip Hale's program book, and some of his remarks are worth repeating here.

My constant aim ever since beginning composition has been to write some American music—i.e., some music which would not naturally have been written in any other country, and which should reflect, or express, certain aspects of the American character, or spirit, as felt by myself.

That spirit, as I see it, is energetic—optimistic—nervous—impatient of restraint—and, in its highest aspect, a mighty protest against the benumbing traditions of the past. This new birth—renaissance—of the human spirit, which is America, is a joyous, wildly shouting demonstration. Plenty of jingoism, vulgarity and "Hurrah boys!" attaches to it, but the spirit of the new-birth underlies all, for him who can see it.

This, to the author's knowledge, is the plainest, clearest, and best definition of the spirit of the new American music. It antedates by about ten years what in the mid-thirties became more or less the common program of a new school of young Americans including among others Roy Harris, Aaron Copland, and William Schuman. Like Gilbert, other composers wished to achieve something with an American flavor and character. Some of them, however, like Paine, Foote, Chadwick, MacDowell, applied to their American titles German romanticism; others like Hadley and Converse composed in the more modern Wagner-Richard Strauss manner; Griffes and most of the Nadia Boulanger school used Debussy's impressionistic methods; still others were interested in Stravinsky's neo-classicism, in Schönberg's twelve-tone mysteries, in Hindemith's contrapuntal feats. No doubt estimable works of art can grow, and sometimes have grown, from these imported seeds, but the label "American" attaches to them only in a limited sense. Gilbert, on the other hand, was ready to sacrifice some of the foreign refinements and replace them by a vigorous, even commonplace, utterance, provided he could attain a peculiarly American tang and flavor.

Philip Hale had the right understanding of Gilbert when he wrote in the *Boston Herald*, February 27, 1926, on the Symphonic Piece as follows:

As many of us delight in Walt Whitman's "barbaric yawp" knowing his conscientiousness as an artist which led him to constant filing and revision, so we exult in this hilarious, screaming, exciting outburst of Mr. Gilbert's rugged Muse. No one but an American, regardless of traditions, free from European influence and academic conventionalism, could have written this music.

Olin Downes has also paid tribute to Gilbert's American art, in a remarkable essay published in the *Musical Quarterly*, 1918.

The culmination of Gilbert's career was reached when his orchestral work "The Dance in Place Congo" was performed at the International Festival in Frankfurt, in July 1927. It represented modern American production, along with Copland's "Music for the Theatre." Gilbert's Symphonic Piece is the only one of his compositions to be found in Koussevitzky's programs, however. This regrettable fact may be explained by the composer's untimely death in 1928.

The American public has been too little reminded of Gilbert's achievement in national American music since his departure from the scene of action. Other, younger, and very active personalities have pressed forward and claimed increasing attention. The pioneer Gilbert has been forgotten; yet during his lifetime six of his scores besides the Symphonic Piece were performed by the Boston Symphony Orchestra between 1911 and 1924. The earliest of these was "Comedy Overture on Negro Themes," which Toscanini revived in 1942, after more than thirty years' neglect.

The name of Rubin Goldmark occurs for the last time on a Boston program on October 19, 1928, when Koussevitzky performed "A Negro Rhapsody." Earlier orchestral works by Goldmark heard in Boston were his Overture to "Hiawatha" in 1900 and 1906, and his tone poem "Samson" in 1914. Rubin Goldmark (1873–1936) was the nephew of the famous composer Karl Goldmark. Born in New York, he was educated at the Vienna Conservatory. Back in America he continued his studies with Bruno Oscar Klein and Dvořák. In time Goldmark himself became a renowned teacher of composition, in later years teaching at the Juilliard school of music. His "Negro Rhapsody," based on seven beautiful Negro tunes, is worked out in symphonic style with considerable polyphonic elaboration in the statement, dialogue, and combination of the various themes. One can trace this composition back to Dvořák's maxims concerning the importance of indigenous folk music. In other compositions, the overture to "Hiawatha" and a Requiem based upon Lincoln's Gettysburg Address, he again turned his attention to American topics and American thematic material.

Harold Morris is one of the few composers hailing from the West who have made their way to the Boston Symphony. Born in San Antonio, Texas, and a graduate of the University of Texas, Morris continued his professional studies with Stillman Kelley, Godowsky, Scalero, and others. During the twenties quite a number of Morris' works were performed by major American orchestras and chamber-music groups. His trio and string quartet were even included in the few American works submitted to the jury in Europe making final selections for a festival of the International Society of Contemporaneous Music. After this promising start, however, the music of Morris has lately been absent from most programs of the more important musical events in America. His name is recorded a single time in the Boston programs, on October 23, 1931, when he played his own Piano Concerto. In the concerto large use is made of Negro music, the "rugged, rhythmic character of the African negro drumbeat," as well as the beautiful spiritual "Pilgrim's Song" and other Southern folksong material.

George Gershwin, before reaching Boston, had already been famous for many years in the world of musical comedy, jazz, and popular songs. Radio and records had carried his music far into the world. "Rhapsody in Blue" had made a hit even in Europe, when Paul Whiteman and his band gave sensational concerts in Berlin and other European cities in 1924, and Gershwin played his Rhapsody with them. The author can testify to the enthusiasm awakened by Gershwin and his Rhapsody in Berlin, as he had the privilege of writing the German version of Whiteman's program books. Gershwin did not come to Boston until January 29, 1932, when he played his Rhapsody No. 2, with orchestra. This was not the "Rhapsody in Blue," but a new score, recently written in California. It originally had the queer title "Rhapsody in Rivets"; subsequently Gershwin substituted the modest and unpretentious title "No. 2." In 1925 and 1928, it was Walter Damrosch who introduced Gershwin's Piano Concerto and "An American in Paris" in serious symphonic programs, thus setting an example later followed by other famous orchestras.

Gershwin's Piano Concerto appeared on a Boston program

rather late, on October 6, 1939, as a part of two programs of exclusively American music selected by Koussevitzky. At Arthur Fiedler's Pops Concerts the Gershwin Concerto had already been heard three times, once played by Gershwin himself, twice by Sanromá; when Koussevitzky conducted, the solo part was performed by Abram Chasins. The style of the concerto is a mixture of jazz, Charleston rhythms, and blues with genuine symphonic writing—a mixture not devoid of a peculiar charm, and certainly unique. Hardly any one but Gershwin could have concocted such a musical brew with equally good flavor.

The last Gershwin work so far heard at a Boston Symphony Orchestra concert was music from the opera *Porgy and Bess,* conducted by Richard Burgin on November 26, 1943. It was arranged as "A Symphonic Picture" by Robert Russell Bennett. Owing to this skillful arrangement these exciting and insinuating tunes of Gershwin have gained access to the serious programs of symphony concerts.

Carl McKinley (b. 1895) is represented only once in a Boston Symphony program, on January 16, 1931, when his composition "Masquerade" was performed, with Henry Hadley as guest conductor. The composer took up his musical career in Boston, after studies at Harvard University and in New York, Paris, Munich, and Italy. A well-known and highly esteemed organist and teacher, McKinley is ranked among Boston's best resident musicians. "Masquerade," written in 1924, had been widely performed in various American cities before it reached Boston's Symphony Hall. Its title refers to the masquerading of the theme in a chain of loosely strung variations. This composition is written somewhat in the manner of Schumann's "Carnaval," but is treated in the style of up-to-date, brilliant, and showy American dance music. Written for a large modern orchestra with no instrument omitted, "Masquerade" has great popular appeal and has been successful.

Leo Sowerby (b. 1895) is a composer much better known in his native city of Chicago and in the mid-western states than in Boston and New York. His name appears on the Boston programs only three times: on March 11, 1932, when Koussevitzky conducted his poem for orchestra "Prairie"; in 1937, when his piano concerto was played; and in 1938 when his organ concerto was heard. Yet from about 1915 and all through the twenties, at a time when his present well-known younger rivals were just commencing their careers, Sowerby was considered one of the most promising progressive American composers. Sowerby was in 1919 the first winner of the American Prix de Rome, which had just been established. At the memorable first International Festival in Salzburg, 1922, Sowerby was the only American representative—he performed his violin sonata—besides the more European than American Ernest Bloch.

As Sowerby settled in Chicago, this city naturally became the center of his activities. A certain rivalry and jealousy in music has always existed between Chicago and the Eastern cities, similar to the competition of Berlin and Leipzig, or to that of Berlin and Munich. At Chicago, a mid-western school of composition grew up around the Chicago Symphony Orchestra, just as a New England and a New York school were fostered by the Boston Symphony and the New York Philharmonic. Many of the Chicago favorites were little known in Boston, the only composer who enjoyed home rights there being John Alden Carpenter, in part because of his Harvard background.

In the *Boston Transcript* of March 10, 1932, Alfred H. Meyer introduced Sowerby to the musical public of Boston. He mentioned that Sowerby had explored all factors in modern musical method, including jazz in two works for Paul Whiteman's orchestra, and modern harmonic devices in his Second Symphony and in "Prairie." He also spoke of the "indigenously American" background of his music, lauded his "exuberance of spirit, an exuberance so great that it carried a definite originality inevitably in its train." This praise, however, was strangely contradicted by Meyer's final dictum that "this originality sometimes amounts to nothing more or less than waywardness."

A new work of Sowerby rather exceptionally had its first performance at Boston, when the eminent Boston organist E. Power Biggs played Sowerby's Concerto for Organ and Orchestra, on April 22, 1938. As Sowerby is himself an accomplished organist, one might have expected the organ part to be brilliant and effectively written—and it was. But the three movements in themselves are interesting from a symphonic point of view. The vigorous first movement in sonata form in C major is followed by a "slow and wistful" piece in the distant key of E flat minor. The structural plan of this second movement is unusual and ingenious. The orchestra and the organ each elaborates its own theme; the organ working out one in fugato manner, while the orchestra simultaneously develops another. The finale, marked "boldly, moderately fast," commences with a fantasy-like introduction and cadenza, leading over to the principal theme. The five variations of this theme are not, as is usual in such cases, separate pieces, but follow continuously, each joined to another by a transitional interlude.

CHAPTER 7

ILLUSTRATIVE AMERICAN
PROGRAM MUSIC

A number of gifted American composers who wrote program music were also active in other fields. Discussion of them will, therefore, occasionally include references to their other works as well as to their programmatic compositions.

Between 1900 and 1930 Frederick Converse (1871–1940) was one of Boston's best-known musicians. He was one of the rare American composers who could boast of several operas performed by the New York Metropolitan Opera and the now deceased Boston Opera. Before Koussevitzky's arrival the Boston Symphony Orchestra had played half a dozen of his orchestral works. The new conductor could not bypass a Boston musician of so considerable a reputation, and accordingly four works by Converse appeared on Koussevitzky's programs, between 1927 and 1935.

On April 15, 1927, Koussevitzky conducted the first performance of a queer orchestral fantasy by Converse, entitled *"Flivver Ten Million, A Joyous Epic* (Inspired by the familiar legend 'The ten millionth Ford is now serving its owner')." Here is a curious exhibition of Americanism. The composer acknowledges in the program book that "Pacific 231" by Honegger awoke in him the desire of competing with the skillful Parisian musician. He might have added that Prokofieff's satiric and burlesque pieces, Stravinsky's "Petrouchka," and Richard Strauss's descriptive "Alpen Symphonie" also acted as conscious or unconscious models in the depths of his mind. Perhaps one could regard this score as being a clever joke, and accordingly concede that it has artistic merit. The question arises, however, whether so banal a program justifies the gigantic orchestral apparatus employed and the amount of labor spent on it. Comparing Saint-Saëns' witty "Carnaval des Animaux" with "Flivver," one easily perceives the difference between genuine fun, exquisite wit, spontaneous, imaginative humor and exaggerated artificial burlesque.

Without its long program, Converse's "Flivver" would be incomprehensible. Thanks to it, we know at least what the composer wished to suggest by his music. "Chanticleer announcing dawn, as the city of Detroit stirs at sunrise; the factory whistles and bells, calling to labor; the Din of the Builders, expressed by fugal factory noises; the Birth of the Hero, as the new car enters its life of service, but also of adventure. America's Romance—America's Frolic—America's Tragedy," described acoustically in the sections "May Night by the Roadside—The Joy-Riders—The Collision." The typical American happy ending is provided in the finale, where the repaired car "proceeds . . . with redoubled energy, typical of the indomitable spirit of America." The immense orchestra adds to its usual forces an organ, automobile horn, wind machine, anvil, and a whole brigade of percussion instruments.

Like Honegger's "Pacific 231," Converse's "Flivver" aroused the American instinct for sport, and dozens of papers in many states related the story of this composition. Special reports were carried even to readers as far as Tennessee and Florida.

In the following season, 1927–1928, another new work by Converse was introduced by Koussevitzky. The tone poem "California" performed on April 6, 1928, tries, as did "Flivver," to awaken impressions of American life and scenery by translating into music an elaborate descriptive program. On a visit to California Converse had witnessed the Fiesta in Santa Barbara, a procession illustrating various phases of civilization in Southern California. This experience resulted in a suite of pieces, based on the following program: Victory Dance of the first Inhabitants, with reminiscences of Indian dances and their peculiar tunes—Spanish Padres and Explorers, expanding motives from an old Latin hymn and culminating in a brilliant march, suggestive of the Conquistadores—The March of Civilization, the establishment of the missions—Land of Poco Tiempo, with dreamy Spanish tunes, the soft music of guitars and mandolins, the sleepy tolling of mission bells—Invasion of the Gringos, a boisterous, rough

episode, with use of a rollicking Yankee sailor song, "The Cape
Cod Chanty" and an Iowa folksong, "The Unconstant Lover"—
Midnight at "El Paseo," 1927, where Spanish song and dance is
mixed with modern jazz. This program might better serve for
the music of a ballet or motion picture than for a work of symphonic art. In its way, it is American, but it represents an earlier,
more primitive type of Americanism in music than that professed
by the leaders of the present time. Yet Converse's score is brilliantly written, and if it were not so pretentious in its demands
on the orchestra, it might well be applauded in a popular symphony concert.

The shortcomings of this piece are of an aesthetic rather than
technical nature. Its lack of a definite and unified style now
appears objectionable; for the younger American composers have
come to acquire a more acute feeling for the value and importance of a clearly pronounced style. In this acquisition lies the
main progress of American music in the forties as compared with
that of the twenties.

In his symphonic suite "American Sketches," which Koussevitzky introduced on February 8, 1935, Converse added a picturesque and descriptive score to several earlier ones of the same
type. In his notes for the Boston program book he explains that
the four movements "are descriptive in character, but not actually
realistic: suggestions rather than pictures." Such an assertion
seems rather superfluous. How could descriptive music be realistic rather than suggestive? It is utterly beyond the power of music
to give a realistic picture of Manhattan. Though granting that
the first movement, entitled "Manhattan," "expresses the activity
and turmoil of a great city, the grandeur, as well as the sinister
sordidness of its varied scenes," one might just as well call such
a piece London, Paris, Rome, or Babylon.* The second movement, called "The Father of Rivers," might just as well have
illustrated the Nile or the Amazon, had it not interwoven a bit
of local color, an old Negro melody. The third movement, "The

* Vaughan Williams in his "London Symphony" has shown how a
similar problem can be solved with the help of a superior clarified
aesthetic insight and conception.

Chicken Reel," a scherzo, is more convincingly American in character, because it is founded on an "old country-fiddler's tune" that has genuine American flavor. The last movement, "Bright Angel Trail," is "an attempt to portray feelings engendered by the Grand Canyon of Arizona." But it is asking too much of a listener to find in the music a picture of "its mysterious depths, its everchanging lights, its grand vistas and at last a suggestion of the legendary birth of the Hopi Indian race from its profound abyss." These objections are raised more against the muddled, questionable aesthetic conceptions underlying these "American Sketches" than against the music itself, which one may find interesting and enjoyable without pondering its associations with the titles.

Converse's "Prophecy," a tone poem for voice and orchestra, came into existence as the result of a suggestion of Koussevitzky. The composer found his inspiration in the sublime words in the thirty-fourth and thirty-fifth chapters of Isaiah. Converse is at his best in this serious and elevated work, which gave wings to his imagination and his inventive powers. The valuable cantata was sung by Beata Malkin on December 16, 1932, for the first time.

John Alden Carpenter of Chicago first appeared on a Koussevitzky program on December 9, 1927. Yet Carpenter scores had been played by the Boston Symphony Orchestra six times previously, between 1915 and 1924. Indeed Carpenter, born in 1876, a pupil of Professor Paine at Harvard and later of the eminent theorist Bernhard Ziehn in Chicago, was one of the most successful American composers of his epoch, and at the same time a most successful business man.

What has been said above about the recent progress in aesthetic insight, in connection with some of Converse's music, also applies to Carpenter. On December 9, 1927, Koussevitzky performed Carpenter's suite "Adventures in a Perambulator," a piece much liked in its time and frequently heard in many cities. The Boston Symphony Orchestra had already played these "Adventures" three times before Koussevitzky conducted them. Though quite

a number of Carpenter's other scores have appeared in later
Boston programs, "Perambulator" has apparently come to the
close of its career in Boston. The reason may be found in the
gradual change of aesthetic maxims. A complicated score in six
movements, for a tremendous orchestra, devoted to the adventures of an American baby wheeled around by his nurse in his
baby carriage, really does not make much sense at the present
time, though the music is itself not—and undoubtedly has not
been—without charms.

The preface to "Perambulator," in the December 9, 1927, program book, takes no less than sixty-four printed lines to inform
the listener what the music illustrates in its six chapters, entitled:
"En voiture—The Policeman—The Hurdy-Gurdy—The Lake—
Dogs—Dreams." Besides this preface, Carpenter wrote a kind of
musical guide through the adventures in an analytical essay of
forty lines; this also has been reprinted in the Boston program
book.

One can easily see that Richard Strauss's "Sinfonia Domestica"
and parts of Stravinsky's "Petrouchka" have not escaped Carpenter's attention. But what a difference of aesthetic conception
and propriety, and what a difference in the proportions of
subject-matter are found between these two products of a pro-
longed aesthetic tradition in Europe and the American music
"Perambulator"! Yet with all these slips of taste there is plenty
of ingenuity and musical skill wasted on an improper theme.

A second, later work by Carpenter was performed by Koussevitzky along with "Perambulator," on December 9, 1927. "Skyscrapers, a Ballet of American Life," written in 1924, ten years
after "Adventures," shows a considerable advance in aesthetic
maturity. This ballet, originally intended for performance by
Diaghilev at Monte Carlo, was instead given for the first time
by the New York Metropolitan Opera. According to Carpenter's
own statement, his aim was to "reflect some of the many rhythms,
movements and sounds of modern American life." In the music,
as indicated by the scenic actions, one encounters a peculiarity
of American life that "reduces itself to violent alternations of

work and play, each with its own peculiar and distinctive rhythmic character." Accordingly, the ballet presents in six scenes:

1. Symbols of restlessness.
2. An abstraction of the skyscraper, and of the work that produces it—and the interminable crowd that passes by.
3. The transition from work to play.
4. Any "Coney Island" . . . and a few of its manifold activities . . .
5. The return from play to work.
6. Skyscrapers.

This work is not accompanied by long explanatory essays; the listener himself makes out the sense of the music, guided by the brief table of contents just quoted. Based on the idea "work and play," "Skyscrapers" has a theme appropriate for a modern American ballet. And though American materialism and not spirituality inspires the action, the scenery, and the music, this materialism is at least animated. This very effective ballet music must have greatly pleased the Boston public, for between 1927 and 1939 Koussevitzky performed "Skyscrapers" four times.

In one of the Tuesday afternoon concerts, on February 23, 1932, Koussevitzky conducted the first performance of Carpenter's "Song of Faith" for chorus and orchestra. The Cecilia Society Chorus sang the choral part and Clifton J. Furness acted as the speaker. "Song of Faith," which paid homage to the "Father of His Country" at the celebration of George Washington's two hundredth anniversary, is a cantata for chorus and orchestra, on a text prepared by the composer. In eight sections the full chorus alternates with men's voices and women's voices alone. Some of these sections contain allusions to old popular Yankee songs, touching a variety of moods. One of them, an enthusiastic "Song of Freedom" for the full chorus, is followed by sopranos' and altos' singing of how "young Doodle Dandy" came to town. The men's voices respond with a martial strain, reminiscent of a redskins' war cry. Next follows a gentle lullaby, merging into a parting-song from life. Then a Yankee band strikes up a vigorous tune, calling attention to the voice of the "Father." Here Washington speaks, the recitative containing excerpts from Washington's writings, and the full chorus in a spirited stanza brings to

a dignified close this worthy tribute. One can regard this piece
as a precursor of Aaron Copland's "Lincoln Portrait" written
a decade later.

On October 21, 1932, a new work by Carpenter was added to
the preceding list, when Koussevitzky conducted for the first time
a piece called "Patterns," for orchestra and piano obbligato, with
the composer as soloist. This time the title "has no literary or
programmatic significance." The piece shows various "patterns,"
as it progresses from one mood to another. One might call it a
suite of improvisations of varying character in which the orchestral part is just as important as the episodes given over to the
piano, if not more so. In a slow middle episode a solo violin
joins the piano; later waltz rhythms crop up, followed by a hint
of jazz; and an excursion into the Spanish musical domain offers
a colorful contrast to the American background.

In Boston, on January 17, 1937, a new work by Carpenter had
its second performance, the initial one having taken place a few
weeks earlier in Carpenter's home city of Chicago. Entitled
"Danza," this short composition is, according to the composer's
explanation, in its "melodic and rhythmic content a mixture of
Spain and America."

The last work of Carpenter performed by Koussevitzky was a
Concerto for Violin and Orchestra, heard on March 3, 1939.
Zlatko Balokovic, the distinguished Croatian violinist, for whom
the concerto was evidently written, played it in a number of
cities, Boston being the fourth in the series. A special feature of
this score is the huge orchestra opposed to the solo violin; a large
group of percussion instruments, besides celesta, harp, piano,
and bells, are added to the full symphony orchestra, with trombones and tuba. This array of instrumental forces posed a number of rather new problems in a violin concerto. Whether the
composition has emerged victoriously from its problematic status
will be proved only when it gains full admission to the rather
small repertory of modern concertos of our leading violinists.
Such admission is not yet manifest six years after the completion
of the score, however it may appear in the future. Even the most
famous soloists are not too eager to burden themselves with a

new, difficult work of a problematic character, even if such a work should be uncommonly interesting. A brilliant sound effect can be readily conceded to the Carpenter score, written in one continuous movement.

Joseph Deems Taylor (b. 1885) was until the beginning of the thirties one of America's best-known and most highly esteemed composers. As in the case of several other remarkable musicians of the older generation, attention was more and more diverted from him when in the mid-thirties the change of style and taste already mentioned took place. But in the incessant evolution of musical art, composers of any generation must yield the center of public attention to newcomers. The culmination of Taylor's achievements and fame was reached in 1931, when his second opera, *Peter Ibbetson,* was enthusiastically acclaimed at its performance by the New York Metropolitan Opera.

At the Orchestra's concerts only one of Taylor's works has been heard during the two decades of Koussevitzky's leadership: the suite "Through the Looking-glass," performed on January 29, 1932, and partly repeated on October 4, 1939, and December 26, 1941. This piece, written in the years 1917–1921, is program music, like that practiced throughout the twenties in America. The idea behind program music has not always been to tell a specific story, which can be done but crudely in most cases; more enlightened spirits have used a story only as an incentive rather than a pattern for creating a piece of music. Such compositions follow their own law, though covered by titles. Taylor's suite was of this type. His inspiration, or incentive, was the famous book of Lewis Carroll, *Through the Looking Glass.* At the last performance in 1941, which the author attended, Koussevitzky left out two pieces, "Jabberwocky" and "The White Knight." But he included the charming and poetic "Dedication," an expressive, melodious songlike piece in Schumannesque spirit, in which the music tells about the "Child of the pure, unclouded brow and dreaming eyes of wonder" and "loving smile" whose "shadow of a sigh" trembles through the story. In "The Garden of Live Flowers," a graceful scherzando piece "reflects the brisk chatter of the swaying, bright-colored denizens of the garden." In the

piece entitled "Looking-Glass Insects," the many-voiced conver-
sation of various insects gives rise to an amiable, lively, and
clever assembly of queer and slightly comical sonorities. This
refined and fantastic piece was written before ugly burlesque
and parodistic music became the fashion of the day.

For a single time the name of Philip James—who is well
known in New York as chairman of New York University's music
department—is found on a Boston program. On January 20, 1933,
his suite for orchestra "Station WGBZX" was played in a concert
at which Albert Stoessel was guest conductor. The piece had just
achieved sensational success and publicity, winning the five-
thousand-dollar prize offered by the National Broadcasting Company in a nationwide contest, for which no less than five hundred and seventy-three American composers competed. As a
novel procedure in this contest the final award was made not by
a small committee of professional judges, as is usually the case,
but by one hundred and fifty selected listeners from many states.
They judged the radio performance of five scores chosen, from
the mass of entries submitted, by a jury of five prominent musicians: Walter Damrosch, Leopold Stokowski, Frederick Stock,
Tullio Serafin, and Nikolai Sokoloff. The queer title of James's
work is thus easily explained by the nature of the contest and
by its sponsorship by the National Broadcasting Company. The
music presents a sinfonietta in four movements: a piece in sonata
form, followed by a scherzo, a slow movement, and a rondo
finale. These four movements, however, would hardly be intelli-
gible and effective without the detailed literary program which
describes scenes in a radio station. The first, "In the Lobby," is
"meant to portray the corridors of a large broadcasting station."
One hears "the various sounds peculiar to a radio station . . .
the noise and bustle of crowds . . . fragments of voice trials . . .
snatches of a Chinese or Indian program . . . announcements
intermingled with the rhythm of a jazz-band . . . the movement
is, in fact, a kind of radio Grand Hotel."

The scherzo, a burlesque, is entitled "Interference" and utilizes
musically the "distressing moments caused by badly tuned receiv-
ing sets, blanketing of stations, static, etc." Further on, the "voice

of the Robot is introduced . . . crooning a phrase in the popular style . . . bursting into wild, inhuman laughter."

The slow movement, "A Slumber Hour," is a radio nocturne, expressive of "the quietude of a late evening broadcast," and indulging in "the chiming of a bell and solo passages for violin and violoncello."

The finale, called "Mikestruck," is a grotesque rondo in "tempo di Jazz," suggestive "of the unquenchable enthusiasm of the mikestruck amateur, who feels the urge to express himself before the microphone."

James's clever and witty piece is a good specimen of the type of descriptive, literary music that was fashionable in America during the twenties, a type that by 1940 had almost entirely disappeared as a result of the recent change of taste and of aesthetic conceptions. "Station WGBZX" belongs with a number of novel pieces already mentioned that take joy in suggestive tone-painting, lack logical coherence and development, and have structural weakness.

Robert Russell Bennett (b. 1894) has won great fame as a virtuoso of modern orchestration. He has exceptional skill in polishing to a brilliant luster the scores of other less skillful musicians, thus helping them to obtain popular success in the field of stage show and musical comedy. In the programs of major symphony orchestras his name is rarely found; yet he has tried his hand at serious composition repeatedly, with no mean success—at least financially. Bennett has won about every award for which younger musicians compete in America, including a Guggenheim Fellowship. He almost won the super-prize of twenty-five thousand dollars offered by the RCA Victor Company in 1927 for "an outstanding serious composition for orchestra." The judges finally decided to divide the sum into five parts, of which Bennett was awarded two-fifths for the two scores submitted by him. One of these was "Abraham Lincoln—a Likeness in Symphonic Form," the other was "Sights and Sounds." Of Bennett's Lincoln portrait not much has been heard since 1927, considerably less than has been heard of Aaron Copland's "Lincoln Portrait," written in 1940.

"Sights and Sounds" was heard in Boston rather late, fifteen years after its completion, in a concert conducted by Richard Burgin on January 22, 1943. The work, in fact, arrived too late. It was the product of an aesthetic system in vogue at the time when it was written but somewhat outmoded in 1943. The composer's aim was to display "every brilliant and difficult orchestral color of which I could think." This "orchestral entertainment" written "for an enormous band of musicians" has also an enormous background in its seven "sights" and corresponding "sounds." It was meant to picture Union Station, Highbrows, Lowbrows, Electric Signs, Night Club, Skyscraper, Speed. There was indeed an amazing collection of strange, even novel, sonorities to be heard, and the technical skill here displayed may well be admired. But the "outstanding serious composition" demanded by the generous Victor Company has very questionable artistic value. Instead of achieving much with few means—the sign of a true masterpiece—here little is achieved with much, even enormous, means. This case, like so many before, demonstrates the futility of the American idea that one can buy great art or coax it into existence by holding out a big bag of money. What queer ideas of "outstanding serious music" the judges in this competition must have had! "Sights and Sounds" is parallel to pieces like James's "Station WGBZX," Converse's "Flivver Ten Million" and "California," Carpenter's "Adventures in a Perambulator," Whithorne's "Moon Trail," and other ambitious, grandiose exhibitions of an Americanism in music in vogue during the twenties but little relished at the present. The nation's composers have progressed a little in overcoming the materialistic spirit dominant in American music two decades ago.

Robert Russell Bennett's virtuosity is applied to much better advantage in his brilliant and effective arrangement of George Gershwin's *Porgy and Bess* music, which he transformed into a symphonic picture. This interesting and impressive piece was also heard in the concert conducted by Burgin on November 26, 1943.

On April 18, 1930, Koussevitzky performed a composition entitled "Broadway" by Samuel Gardner. This is the only time

Gardner's name appears in a Boston program, in which, unfortunately, the composer refused to comment on his composition.
We are informed by Philip Hale's notes that Gardner, a native
of Russia, came as a child to America before 1900, was a pupil
of Winternitz, Kneisel, and Goetschius in New York, and acquired fame throughout America as a violin virtuoso. The
impressive list of his compositions included a violin concerto, a
string quartet that won a Pulitzer Prize in 1918, "Hebraic Fantasy" for clarinet and string quartet, the symphonic poem "New
Russia," awarded the Loeb Prize in 1918, Piano Quintet, and
many other works. Manifestly Gardner was a highly gifted and
successful musician. Yet for many years his name has been absent
from concert programs.

Like Gardner, Louis Gruenberg—born in 1883 in Russia—came
to America as a child. Unlike Gardner, however, his artistic
career has progressed without interruption to the present time,
and he has become one of the potent forces of Americanism in
music. Many of his earlier years were spent in Europe; and when
the author knew him in Berlin before the first World War,
Gruenberg was recognized as one of Busoni's ablest and most
enthusiastic pupils. During the season 1929–1930 Koussevitzky
performed two of Gruenberg's works. The symphonic poem "The
Enchanted Isle," heard in Boston on November 8, 1929, is according to the composer's explanation in the program book, "a bridge
between the old and the new" in his career. The "old" means his
prewar European background, the "new" his ever-growing interest in an American style. "The Enchanted Isle" in its final form,
published by the Juilliard Foundation, is the second version of
a work dating back to the time of the first World War, which
was thoroughly revised eight years later.

Gruenberg's "Jazz Suite," Opus 28, performed by Koussevitzky
on February 21, 1930, is, as the title indicates, a product of the
composer's newly acquired American phase. The suite has four
movements: Fox-trot Tempo; Boston Waltz Tempo; Blues
Tempo, slow drag; One-step Tempo. Artur Rodzinski, who
conducted this suite in Los Angeles, wrote for the program book

of his concert an extensive explanation and defense of Gruenberg's score and artistic tendency. This spirited defense informs
us that around 1930 many American musicians and music lovers
objected to jazz in a symphony concert, on the grounds that
music of the dance hall and night club was out of place in a
dignified concert program, and Gruenberg is here credited with
ennobling the jazz idiom, assimilating it to the symphonic technique, and enriching it with new rhythmical refinements and
complications.

Gruenberg exploited the symphonic possibilities of jazz in a
number of works. One that was extraordinarily successful was
"Daniel Jazz," much applauded not only in America but also at
European international festivals. Though heard in Symphony
Hall only in 1939, "Daniel Jazz" had been part of a memorable
concert given in 1928 by a chamber orchestra of Boston Symphony players conducted by Koussevitzky's associate conductor,
Richard Burgin. This concert deserves to be called memorable,
since its program contained the first Boston auditions of such
important and highly controversial works as Schönberg's "Pierrot
Lunaire," Stravinsky's Octet, and Hindemith's "Marienlieder."
To be placed on the same program with works of such caliber
was a great compliment to "Daniel Jazz."

The fourth and last work of Gruenberg heard at an Orchestra
concert was Symphony No. 1, Opus 17, performed on February
10, 1933. Although composers usually feel content and proud
when Koussevitzky chooses one of their scores for performance,
Gruenberg seems to have considered the choice of this symphony
unfortunate. In his notes for the program book he laments that
a work written back in 1919 and revised in 1929 should have its
first performance in 1933. He looks back on this score "with
mingled feelings" because it is "so different in feeling, technique
and subject matter to what I do today." Nevertheless, there must
have been something attractive and promising in the score to
recommend it to Koussevitzky's active interest. The up-to-date
point of view is frequently overstressed by composers, who are
inclined to feel somewhat humiliated when an earlier, less mod-

ern work is presented for public discussion. Yet an earlier work may have more freshness of invention, more youthful charm, than a later score in sophisticated, modernistic dress array.

Emerson Whithorne, born in 1884 in Cleveland, belongs to the older group of contemporary American composers. In the twenties his music was generally considered representative of radical American modernism; it was widely performed wherever novelty of musical diction was patronized. His piano suite "New York Nights and Days" was the only work chosen to represent American music at the first festival of the recently founded international Society for Contemporary Music at Salzburg in 1923. In orchestral and jazz arrangements this promenade through New York—on a ferry, in Chinatown, Greenwich Village, Times Square —made Whithorne widely known all over America. Numerous other chamber music and orchestral works of his were played in many cities. Yet not until December 15, 1933, did he gain admission to Boston's Symphony Hall, when Koussevitzky performed his symphonic suite, Opus 53, "Moon Trail." This composition is concerned with landscape impressions received by Whithorne during a visit to California. Its four movements are:

1. "Death Valley," the desert region, destitute of life, with its fiery sands and hot winds, the graveyard of many caravans.

2. "The Devil's Kitchen," an especially hideous spot in the great desert, with its volcanic eruptions, its "scalding jets of hissing steam shot out of boiling caldrons."

3. "Palos Verdes," in welcome contrast to the dreary scenes depicted in the two preceding movements, a picture of luxurious nature, verdant scenery, and languid beauty.

4. "Surf at Malibu," a vigorous finale, inspired by the mighty rhythm of the booming and roaring surf. "Through the clash of storm and wind and sea is heard Neptune's gusty laughter."

This suite, "Dedicated to my friend Serge Koussevitzky," was played from the manuscript and has remained unpublished, like the majority of American efforts at symphonic composition. This makes it difficult, almost impossible in numerous cases, to obtain after many years a first-hand acquaintance with the scores. One has to rely on the comments of critics in the local papers, and even these are difficult to obtain.

It seems significant that most of the American compositions widely known in the twenties have, since about 1933, disappeared from programs almost entirely. The reason may be not primarily a lack of musical interest in these older scores but a fundamental change of taste that took place in the thirties. The elaborate literary, descriptive programs, the exotic themes, landscape impressions, sociological and technological topics, treated for instance in Eichheim's Chinese and Javanese pieces, in Converse's "Flivver" and "California," in Carpenter's "Perambulator" and "Skyscrapers," in Schelling's "Morocco," Josten's "Jungle," Gardner's "Broadway," Hadley's "Streets of Pekin," Deems Taylor's "Through the Looking-Glass," James's "Station WGBZX," Whithorne's "Moon Trail," and many others were not relished any more. The rising, younger generation of American composers was decidedly in favor of a return to "absolute" music, constructive problems, contrapuntal texture, and terse expression. In short, the basic maxims of neo-classicism were interpreted in a variety of individual ways by the new class of younger Americans who began plowing the symphonic field and gradually pushed out of it their immediate predecessors who had desired to reap a different crop. Artists animated by the new creed, men like Roy Harris, Aaron Copland, Randall Thompson, William Schuman, Walter Piston, Howard Hanson, and Samuel Barber took over the leadership. The present time is in the midst of this stylistic tendency, represented by creative artists forty to fifty years of age. But already a still younger generation is making some stir on the American musical scene; musicians like Leonard Bernstein, Lukas Foss, David Diamond, Gail Kubik, Ellis B. Kohs. They have not yet reached their full maturity, but already it is evident that they do not mean to be obedient followers of their immediate predecessors. What the outcome of their young and fresh efforts will be is now being eagerly watched. Yet it can be said that these youngest American composers should not consider it beneath their dignity to become acquainted with at

least a selection of what the older generation of American composers had to offer. From the music of Paine, Foote, Chadwick,
MacDowell, Parker, Hadley, Gilbert, Converse, Hill, and Smith,
they might profitably acquire a sense of careful, clean workmanship, well-balanced form, melodic character, reasonable proportion of the means employed to the dominating idea, and economy
in every respect.

CHAPTER 8

JUDAISM IN
AMERICAN MUSIC

There exist many remarkable exponents of Jewish music, and
the world center for their activities is America. As one speaks of
Judaism in American music, he may use the term in one of two
senses. The term first applies to music animated by a racially
Jewish spirit and composed by Jewish musicians who have acquired home rights in America through long residence here.
Only three composers belonging to this group are represented
in the Boston program: Achron, Bloch, and Jacobi. Judaism in
American music secondly refers to the activities of many highly
gifted American composers of Jewish descent whose works have
contributed to the vitality and growth of American music but
do not stem from racial inspiration. To this group belong such
artists as Gershwin, Gruenberg, Copland, William Schuman,
Leonard Bernstein, and a few others, who are discussed elsewhere.

Joseph Achron, born in Russian Poland in 1886, had acquired
a considerable European reputation as a violinist and composer
before he settled in New York in 1925. In the mass of his theatrical, vocal, chamber, and instrumental solo compositions a
large group is devoted to Hebrew music. An example is his
Violin Concerto, Opus 60, performed by Koussevitzky on January 24, 1927, with Achron as soloist. It was the first of his larger
works written in America. In his notes for the Boston program
book, Achron stated that the first movement is based on elements
of Hebrew synagogue chants, called tropes. Fifteen of these
tropes form the thematic material, used in a very elaborate
manner. "Every passage, every contrapuntal line grows from the
Trope elements. Certain themes, appearing at first in their full
embodiment, are later reduced to skeleton form. Others, on the
contrary, are presented in the beginning briefly and are after-

wards carried to florid completion. Several themes are at times combined. At the end, three of them are sounded simultaneously."

The second movement is likewise based on Hebrew material, this time not of liturgic but of popular type. Two Palestinian dance tunes are treated in what the composer calls a "jugglery" manner. These "Improvisations on two themes of Yemen" begin in the manner of variations and pass over gradually into improvisations. The unorthodox structure of the concerto invites closer study.*

Since 1911 Achron has been a member of the Society for Hebrew Folk Music, which was established in czarist St. Petersburg. In this field he has been one of the most active workers, along with Michael Knessin, Alexander Krein, M. Milner, and others. The activities of this group antedate those of Ernest Bloch, who has become the best-known exponent of Hebrew music.

Ernest Bloch, born in Switzerland, educated there as well as in Brussels, Frankfurt, and Paris, had nothing whatsoever American about him when he first aroused the attention of the Boston public. He came to America in 1916, when he was thirty-six years old and already had considerable repute in Europe as the champion of Jewish music. Since then he has made his home in America, except for frequent periods spent in Europe. His claims as an American composer are founded more on his long residence in this country and on a few works ostensibly doing homage to America than on any really American features of his art. Yet for nearly thirty years his works have appeared more frequently on programs throughout the nation than have those of any native American composer. Although the works of this eminent musician lack genuine Americanism, they cannot be disregarded here; music *in* America is to some extent an inherent part in any survey of music *of* America.

Between 1917 and 1921, Bloch's Two Psalms for Soprano and Orchestra, "Trois Poèmes Juifs," the "Winter-Spring" Poems for Orchestra, and the cello rhapsody "Schelomo" had performances

* Facilitated by the publication of the work by the Universal Edition, Vienna.

at Boston concerts. And so, Bloch was indeed no new name when Koussevitzky arrived. Since then, between 1925 and 1945, the Boston public has heard Bloch's music no less than fifteen times—evidence that this composer's works must have strongly impressed Koussevitzky.

In his second season, 1925–1926, Koussevitzky performed three weighty scores of Bloch. The first of these was the Suite for Viola and Orchestra. In its first version, with piano, the Suite had won the Coolidge Chamber Music Prize in 1919. Half a year later the orchestral version was heard for the first time in New York, and soon afterwards in Paris. There the viola solo was played by Jean Lefranc at a concert in the Conservatory in 1922, and with orchestra by Lefranc at a Colonne concert in 1924. Possibly Koussevitzky attended one or both of these concerts. At any rate, a year later he had imported both Lefranc and the Suite to Boston. Ever since 1925 Lefranc has been the leader of the Boston Orchestra's violas, and the first appearance of this artist as a soloist, on December 11, 1925, was devoted to the Bloch Suite.

Of the Suite and its composer, Philip Hale said that it was "a personal expression, a musical photograph of the man himself . . . a musically psychological document. . . . There are noble measures, there are scornful pages; there is wildness and there is peace in this strange rhapsodic suite . . . it is the music of a man who feels deeply, has worked out his own idiom, has invented his singular, but often effective, impressive orchestration."

The suite, again played by Lefranc, was heard in a Boston concert on November 10, 1944. This time Bloch himself gave a detailed, interesting description of his score in the program book. He excluded the suite from his series of "Jewish works," calling it "rather a vision of the Far East that inspired me: Java, Sumatra, Borneo." The first movement, Lento–Allegro–Moderato, "aims to give the impression of a very wild and primitive Nature." To the "savage cry, like that of a fierce bird of prey," in the Introduction, the viola responds with its meditation. The Allegro opens with "a motive of joyful and perhaps exotic char-

acter" to which the viola responds again, elaborately, leading to
an exciting climax and to a decrescendo "in silence and in slum-
bering mood." The second movement, Allegro ironico, is "a
curious mixture of grotesque and fantastic characters, of sardonic
and mysterious moods." The third movement, Lento, "expresses
the mystery of tropical nights." The last movement, Molto vivo,
is "probably the most cheerful thing I ever wrote." Reminiscences
of the other movements especially fill the lyric intermezzo, in a
"broad and passionate mood." *

The second Bloch work heard in 1925–1926 was the Concerto
Grosso, which had been completed only a few months earlier.
Written for string orchestra and piano, it was originally intended
as a practice piece for the students of the Cleveland Conservatory, of which Bloch was director at that time. Various conductors
were eager to perform it immediately, and it was heard in Cleveland, Los Angeles, Chicago, and Philadelphia before it reached
Boston on December 24, 1925. In this score Bloch followed the
trend away from the sonata form to the older, eighteenth-century
type of concerto used by Bach and Handel—a trend that had
arisen in the early twenties, particularly in Germany. Needless
to say, Bloch's concerto utilized the simpler structural idea of the
concerto grosso not in an antiquarian but in a thoroughly modern spirit. A "piano obbligato" has an important part in this
concerto, reminding the listener of the indispensable cembalo in
eighteenth-century concerted music. Unlike the old cembalo,
however, Bloch's piano is not satisfied with the subordinate function of filling in the harmony, but contributes greatly to the
brilliant effect of the score. The work contains four movements:
an energetic prelude; a grave, elegiac dirge; a more cheerful
pastorale and rustic dances; and as a finale a strong, brisk and
much involved fugue. Jesús María Sanromá, who had recently
been appointed permanent pianist of the Boston Orchestra,
made one of his earliest appearances in the Bloch concerto.

* A detailed appraisal of this suite may be found in Mr. Paul Rosen-
feld's *Musical Chronicle: 1917–1923* (Harcourt, Brace and Company,
New York), chapter ix. This informative account was reprinted in the
Boston program book, December 11, 1925.

Philip Hale showed only a moderate interest in the greater part of the concerto, but had the highest praise for the dirge, in which he heard "the wailing of an oppressed race, not any selfish expression of individual grief. Here . . . is the cry of agony, as of the persecuted, weeping and groaning by the historic wall."

A few months later, on April 16, 1925, Koussevitzky performed the third Bloch score of the season, "Trois Poèmes Juifs." These three pieces, written in 1913, mark the beginning of Bloch's Hebraic phase that also includes musical versions of Psalms 22, 114, and 137, the symphony "Israel," the fantasy "Schelomo," the "Baal Shem" suite for violin and orchestra, and the "Sacred Service." Karl Muck had in 1917 conducted the first Boston performance of "Trois Poèmes," and Bloch wrote for the program book an indispensable explanation of the psychological background of his art.

It is not my purpose, nor my desire, to attempt a "reconstitution" of Jewish music, or to base my work on melodies more or less authentic. I am not an archaeologist. I hold it of first importance to write good, genuine music, *my* music. It is the Jewish soul that interests me, the complex, glowing, agitated soul, that I feel vibrating throughout the Bible: the freshness and naïveté of the Patriarchs, the violence that is evident in the prophetic books; the Jew's savage love of justice; the despair of the Preacher in Jerusalem; the sorrow and the immensity of the Book of Job; the sensuality of the Song of Songs.

All this is in us; all this is in me, and it is the better part of me. It is all this that I endeavor to hear in myself and to transcribe in my music: the venerable emotion of the race that slumbers way down in our soul.

Here is the key to Bloch's music, one that opens not only the Jewish cycle but also the rest of his music, including those works without specific Jewish titles. Bloch went on to say that the "Poèmes" were "the first work of a new period; they consequently have not the maturity of the 'Psalms' or of 'Israel.'" These latter works and "Schelomo" he considers more representative, because "they come from the passion and the violence that I believe to be characteristics of my nature." He adds a few brief remarks on the contents of the three pieces:

I. *Danse*. This music is all in the coloring; coloring rather sombre, mystical, languorous.

II. *Rite*. This movement is more emotional; but there is something solemn and distant, as the ceremonies of a cult.

III. *Cortège Funèbre*. This is more human. My father died—these "poems" are dedicated to his memory. There is something implacably severe in the rhythms that obstinately repeat themselves. At the end, sorrow bursts forth, and at the idea of an eternal separation the soul breaks down. But a very simple and serene melody arises from the orchestral depths as a consolation, a balm, a gentle faith. The memory of our dear departed ones is not effaced; they live forever in our hearts.

The form is free, but it is really there, for I believe that our constitution demands order in a work of art.

In 1917 the Boston musical public heard that type of Jewish music for the first time, and it would be interesting to know what its reaction was. One must conclude that the impression made was considerable, because Koussevitzky included Bloch's "Poèmes" four times in his programs between 1925 and 1939. H. T. Parker's review in the *Boston Evening Transcript*, March 24, 1917, had these headlines: "Strange and Signal Music of Ernest Bloch—Three Jewish Poems that Evoke a Composer of Remarkable Idiom and Procedure, Invention, Imagination and Power—Pieces of a Stinging Vehemence." In the program book of March 17, 1939, Bloch added a much more detailed description. It is not a technical analysis but one of the most revealing documents to be found anywhere concerning the deepest thoughts of an eminent composer on the sources of his art.

Bloch's contribution for the Boston season 1927–1928 consisted of a new manuscript score, "Four Episodes for Chamber Orchestra," performed on December 29, 1927. String quintet, woodwinds, and one horn render the four pieces entitled: "Humoresque Macabre—Obsession—Calm—Chinese." This fanciful score had just been awarded a New York Chamber Music Society prize —Bloch has been exceptionally fortunate in competitions. Even the titles "Humoresque Macabre" and "Obsession" are extremely characteristic of Bloch. Though well received in Boston, the "Episodes" remain isolated; they are not generally counted among Bloch's major works.

Koussevitzky conducted Bloch's "Schelomo" in the season 1929–1930. This Hebrew rhapsody was heard four times at Boston concerts; the first time in April 1923, when Monteux was still conducting the Orchestra. The soloist was Jean Bedetti, who has presided at the first desk of the Boston cello section for nearly twenty-five years. At the second performance, on December 27, 1929, Felix Salmond was the soloist; and at repetitions on December 15, 1935, and January 27, 1939, Bedetti and Piatigorsky played the impressive and grateful solo part. "Schelomo" has become perhaps Bloch's best-known work. It is without doubt the most valuable addition to modern violoncello literature since Dvořák's Concerto was written nearly fifty years ago.

This gorgeous, fantastic composition is a real rhapsody. It is lyric, epic, dramatic, declamatory, passionate and fatalistic, sensuous and ascetic all at once; reconciling all its different moods in an ecstasy and yet sincerity of oriental diction which is distinctly Hebrew rather than Moorish or Arabian. An excellent appreciation of "Schelomo," written by the Italian critic Guido Gatti, was published in the *Musical Quarterly,* January 1921. A second noteworthy description was made by Lawrence Gilman, well-known commentator of the Philadelphia and later the New York Philharmonic program books. It was reprinted in Philip Hale's Boston program book of 1929–1930.

After more than a decade devoted to Hebrew music, Ernest Bloch turned his attention to his new homeland with his epic rhapsody "America" in 1928. In response to *Musical America's* symphony contest Bloch sent in this work. After reviewing the ninety-two manuscript scores submitted, the five judges—among America's most famous conductors, Walter Damrosch, Alfred Hertz, Serge Koussevitzky, Frederick Stock, and Leopold Stokowski—awarded the prize unanimously to Bloch's work. The judges also fixed—a unique distinction—the same dates, December 20, 21, for "America's" first performances in New York, San Francisco, Boston, Chicago, and Philadelphia.

An extensive essay on this symphony, taken over into the Boston program from the *New York Times* of November 11, 1938, explains Bloch's intentions. The composer's dedication reads as follows: "This symphony has been written in love for this country. In reverence to its past, in faith in its future, it is dedicated to the memory of Abraham Lincoln and Walt Whitman, whose vision upheld its inspiration." Accordingly, "America's" three movements are concerned with reminiscences of the country's history. The first movement deals with 1620, "The Soil —The Indians—England—The Mayflower—The Landing of the Pilgrims." The second movement recalls the Civil War, 1861– 1865, and is entitled "Hours of Joy—Hours of Sorrow." The finale, 1926, tells of "The Present—The Future." *

Here is Bloch's contribution to American music. The score is filled with direct allusions to the American scene and atmosphere, as it draws upon hymn tunes, English tunes, Indian songs and dances, Southern plantation melodies, Virginia reels and hornpipes, Stephen Foster songs, and in the finale even jazz. Here, too, is outspoken program music, somewhat like Converse's "California." But whereas Converse composed a picturesque suite with little coherence, Bloch applies a vastly greater symphonic art that unifies all three movements, while dramatizing them. An "anthem" is the germ as well as the culmination of the entire symphony, and the wealth of thematic material is developed, combined, and contrasted by the hand of a master. There can be no doubt that in composing "America" Bloch made a supreme effort to pay worthy homage to his adopted country, just as in another memorable work he honored his native country ("Helvetia," a tone poem, first heard in Boston on March 20, 1939). For all that, "America" has not taken root as deeply as some of the Hebraic works of Bloch. The only repetition of "America" in Boston was on March 17, 1939, when the composer himself conducted. The Boston program book of that date contains a detailed analysis of "America" by Alfred H. Meyer.

After an absence of several years Bloch returned to the Boston scene in March 1939, when Koussevitzky yielded the baton to

---

* In this historical review one misses the Revolution and George Washington, but as a musical work of art need not aspire to the chronological exactness of a historical essay, we must be content with this incomplete musical story.

him for an entire week. At the regular Friday and Saturday concerts, at a Monday concert, and at a Harvard concert in Sanders Theatre, Bloch performed programs made up exclusively of his own works. Among them were two works previously performed, "Trois Poèmes Juifs," the epic rhapsody "America," and also compositions that until then were unknown in Boston. "Two Symphonic Interludes" had their first concert performance on March 17, 1939. They are part of Bloch's opera *Macbeth*, which had a successful start in Paris, back in 1910. It had a run of sixteen performances at the Opera Comique, then disappeared from view for twenty-eight years, and was revived in Naples at the San Carlo Theatre in 1938. The Naples performances probably turned Bloch's attention to the long-forgotten opera score, and he extracted from it, for use in the concert hall, two symphonic interludes.

The first one, heard in the opera during the change of scenery between scene one and two in the first act, pictures "the atmosphere of drunken ambition" prevalent when Macbeth has been persuaded by Lady Macbeth to win the throne for himself by murder. The Wagnerian method of characteristic leitmotives, used throughout the opera, is here adopted by Bloch and serves, by its concatenation and opposition of the various motives, to paint and at the same time to interpret the dominant mood. In the last part of this interlude the agitation subsides, and the music suggests the calm in King Duncan's palace before the crime is committed.

The other interlude is the second intermezzo in the opera's third act; it leads over from the first scene, the Witches' Cavern, to the final scene. The music comprehends wide contrasts, from Macbeth's exultation to doubt, remorse, fear, and despair. Bloch's dynamic, emotionally charged music represents a phase of modern music basically different from the constructivist approach of the Stravinsky school. His attitude is that it is not sufficient to be an excellent craftsman—a goal satisfying for many young neo-classical modernists—but that the composer should also be a poet in tones. This conviction of Bloch is expressed most convincingly in the second description of his

"Poèmes Juifs" published in the Boston program book of March 17, 1939, a document of prime importance for proper appreciation of Bloch's art. No less revealing is Olin Downes's report of an extended interview with Bloch, published in the *New York Times*, January 22, 1939. Extracts from it in the Boston program book above are extremely informative as to Bloch's ideas on a really living art of counterpoint, which he bases on the vocal art of the great Netherlandish and Italian masters of the sixteenth century.

A new major work by Bloch, a Concerto for Violin and Orchestra, was played in 1938 and 1939 by the famous violinist Joseph Szigeti in Cleveland and London, and reached Boston on January 5, 1940. Bloch had been working intermittently on the score for years, and there is no doubt that he considers this violin concerto one of his principal achievements. The author regrets that he had but one chance to get acquainted with this exacting work; for the effort of following the intricacies of the structure, the closely interwoven thematic texture, the coherence of the apparently rhapsodic threads of melody was too great to permit a satisfactory total impression. A much closer acquaintance with so pretentious a score is needed in order to get a sufficiently clear impression of its contents. What the composer has to say on his work, in the Boston program book, emphasizes this concerto's complexity and would be much more serviceable to a student of the score than attendance at the first—and thus far only—performance. Bloch tells us that in the Concerto for once there is "no Jewish inspiration or intention." He even tells us that the principal theme of the first movement is "undoubtedly of an American-Indian character," and that it "probably influenced the atmosphere of, at least, the first two movements." Yet, in spite of this Indian surface, a Jewish accent is subconsciously noticed by a listener familiar with it. Since its first appearance in 1940 the score has not been played. This does not mean, however, that it has been a failure. It will emerge from its temporary oblivion in more propitious times of peace, when great and serious problems of art will again receive the respect and detailed study due them.

Koussevitzky has done full justice to Bloch, as one of the few internationally eminent composers of our time, yet one of Bloch's principal and most impressive works, the symphony "Israel," has never been heard in Boston. This is all the more surprising as "Israel" dates back to 1917. Only recently, in January 1946, a performance by the New York Philharmonic-Symphony Orchestra, conducted by Artur Rodzinski, proved that after more than twenty-five years, at an age when most modern pieces have lost their freshness and immediate appeal, Bloch's "Israel" score still has plenty of vitality. The neglect of this important work should be remedied in Boston.

A second work by Frederick Jacobi, whose "Indian Dances" have been described in a former chapter, was performed by Koussevitzky on April 22, 1943. This "Ode" for orchestra is one of a number of compositions inspired by the Bible and the Jewish temple service. A prayer in the Hebrew Morning Sabbath Service, "O Lord, open thou my lips, and my mouth shall declare thy praise," suggested to the composer musical treatment, even without the words. And, indeed, the stirring and sublime text has "opened the lips" of the musician and has enabled him to declare the Lord's praise in a deeply felt, eloquent, and highly expressive chant, full of religious spirit and noble melody in its varying moods closely following the words of the prayer. Here one sees Jacobi pursuing the path first blazed by Ernest Bloch.

CHAPTER 9

THE RUSSIAN–AMERICAN SCHOOL
—AND OTHERS

One can consider that a Russian-American school of music has existed since about 1925. It consists of a number of Russian musicians, born around 1900 or a little later, who found refuge and permanent homes in America after the Russian Revolution. In this group are Vladimir Dukelsky, Nicolai Berezowsky, Nicolas Lopatnikoff, Arkady Dubensky, and Boris Koutzen, as well as Joseph Achron, who has already been mentioned. They are all interested in absolute music, symphony, concerto grosso, neo-classicism, and illustrative program music has no charms for them. Although their music is decidedly modern, most of them make no attempt to foster an American spirit. That Koussevitzky is especially interested in these gifted compatriots is not surprising. In this group also Bohuslav Martinu may best be included, though he hails not from Russia but from Czechoslovakia.

Vladimir Dukelsky, like Joseph Achron, belongs to the group of Russian musicians who arrived in America about the same time as Koussevitzky. A pupil of Glière in Moscow and a student at the Kiev Conservatory, the talented Dukelsky was fortunate in finding speedy recognition of his achievements. In 1920, at the age of seventeen, he fled from the turmoil of the Russian Revolution to Constantinople; two years later he came to New York where he made an unsuccessful debut as a composer; then he quit America for Paris. There he attracted the attention of Diaghilev, the famous director of the Russian Ballet. In a London interview published in the *Observer* of November 8, 1925, Diaghilev mentioned his discovery of Dukelsky, whom he called the younger brother of his two older protégés, Stravinsky and Prokofieff. The result of this discovery was the music that Dukelsky wrote for the ballet "Zéphyr et Flore," which Diaghilev produced with considerable success in Monte Carlo, Paris, Berlin, and London in 1925. Koussevitzky became interested in the uncommon talent of the young Russian musician and included a suite from the ballet in his program of April 29, 1927. Moreover, he published the piano score of the ballet in his Edition Russe de Musique. In later years the name of Dukelsky has appeared six times on Boston Symphony programs.

After his sojourn in Paris, Dukelsky returned to New York to live, and of all the Russian immigrants who have arrived in America in the last twenty years, he has best succeeded in Americanizing himself. Quickly he acquired the melodic and rhythmic swing of Broadway's musical comedies. He even Americanized his name, and as Vernon Duke became a prosperous Broadway specialist. Yet commercial temptations did not estrange him completely from his original artistic ideals. He continued on a side line his career as a symphonic composer, and in this capacity he remained Vladimir Dukelsky, as before. That Duke should earn plenty of royalties, enabling Dukelsky "to go on with his operas and symphonies," is his guiding maxim. And needless to say Koussevitzky has been mainly interested in the efforts of Dukelsky, rather than those of Duke.

On March 15, 1929, Koussevitzky brought to Boston Dukelsky's First Symphony in F major, which he had introduced in one of his Paris concerts, on June 14, 1928. An Adagio movement from a never finished ballet, ordered by Diaghilev and begun in Florence, was incorporated in this symphony even though Diaghilev had called the piece "too frivolous and Italian in spirit."

Dukelsky's Second Symphony, brought out by Koussevitzky on April 25, 1930, is probably the only symphony written in the unusual key of D flat major. The composer was content with only three movements, the middle one being a rather slow minuet. The finale begins in the character of the Spanish dance *zapateado,* with its castagnetti accompaniment; this is interrupted by an andante episode in alternation with the Spanish theme, which is now presented in scherzando manner; and in conclusion there is a modified return of the principal theme of the first movement. This symphony was chosen to represent American music (along with George Gershwin's "An American in Paris") at the festival of the International Society for Contemporary Music, held at Oxford and London in July, 1931.

Dukelsky made another appearance on April 15, 1932, with an "Epitaph" for soprano solo, chorus, and orchestra, a new work written in 1931 and inscribed "On the Death of Diaghilev." It was meant as a tribute of thanks to the great master of ballet, who years before had discovered Dukelsky's talent and introduced him to the world of music and the theater, and who, in Dukelsky's own words, "brought the sweet breath of Renaissance to the first quarter of our century." The music is written to the words of a poem by the Russian poet Ossip Mandelstamm. The poem paints a winter scene in czarist St. Petersburg; a crowd of fashionable people, leaving the theater late at night, wait for their coachmen to take them home in their sleighs. The close extols the charms of Italian singing—the southern "swallow"—but praises still more the native Russian tongue. Although there is not the slightest reference to Diaghilev in the poem, the composer chose it because it seemed to fit Diaghilev's mentality, with its mixture of longing for Italy and love for Russia.

A strange opus of Dukelsky had its first performance on December 16, 1938, "Dédicaces" for piano, orchestra, and woman's voice obbligato. The composer was fortunate in having so reliable a friend as Koussevitzky to conduct this work, otherwise he might have faced great difficulties in securing the performance of this pretentious and complex composition, which reverses the usual relation of the solo voice to the accompanying instrumental body. There is an elaborate symphonic piano concerto in three movements, with a prologue and epilogue, accompanied by a soprano voice, singing or reciting a series of French poems by the Parisian poet Guillaume Apollinaire. The three principal movements, entitled "À la ville—À la campagne —À la mer," are inspired by the poet's impressions of the city, the countryside, and the sea. The solo voice—decidedly subordinate to the piano and the orchestra—serves as a sort of *conferencier,* explaining in sophisticated French verses the emotional contents of the piece. The structural idea underlying this work is novel and interesting but has proved to be impracticable and ineffective. The degraded vocal part, sung by Marguerite Porter, was a thankless task, all the more so as the sophisticated French poetry could hardly be understood even by those possessing a good knowledge of French. It is a pity that a concerto so interesting in many ways as an instrumental work was gravely hurt in its effect by the composer's whimsical idea, one possibly suggested by the narrator in Stravinsky's Oedipus drama.

Dukelsky's Violin Concerto, dedicated to Ruth Posselt, was played by her for the first time in a concert conducted by Burgin, March 19, 1943. This work is another of the numerous, only partially successful, attempts made in America for twenty years to produce a new violin concerto able to sustain popularity. Full of attractive and interesting details, like all Dukelsky's music, it somehow fails to integrate these details into a convincing unit of a higher order.

Of Dukelsky's new Violoncello Concerto (played for the first time by Piatigorsky on January 4, 5, 1946) it might be said that it is interesting in details, but not sufficiently impressive as a whole. The music exaggerates color at the expense of structure, thus repeating once more a pattern recurring in most of Dukelsky's symphonic scores. There is no lack, however, of brilliant episodes, stretches of romantic lyricism, and in the finale one is reminded of Tchaikovsky's exuberant and almost aggressive march rhythms. Piatigorsky's eminent virtuosity presented the pretentious piece to the best possible advantage.

A new name in American music made its first appearance on March 16, 1931—Nicolai Berezowsky. A young Russian musician from Leningrad, Berezowsky had in the twenties, like many of his countrymen, found his way to New York, there to continue his study of composition with Rubin Goldmark and to become a member of the Philharmonic Symphony Orchestra. His talent for composition was soon recognized, and about 1930 his compositions appeared on programs of modern music. Koussevitzky became interested in the gifted young Russian, and between 1931 and 1945 eight extensive works of Berezowsky were heard in

Boston, including no less than four symphonies and three concertos—for violin, viola, and violoncello. His First Symphony was played in one of the secondary Tuesday evening concerts, on March 16, 1931, and the young composer was invited to conduct his own work; evidently Koussevitzky wanted to try out the new composer's powers and attractiveness before he accorded him the seal of full approval by conducting a Berezowsky score himself. Nobody familiar with Berezowsky's career would have expected to find marked American traits in his music; in fact his First Symphony cannot conceal its Russian origin. But it also evinces a strong creative talent.

After a successful Boston debut with his First Symphony, Nicolai Berezowsky became a regular and welcome guest in Boston. In the following season his Violin Concerto, Opus 14, was heard on December 4, 1931, when Richard Burgin conducted and Berezowsky himself played the solo part.*

For Berezowsky, as well as for a number of other composers, good relations with Koussevitzky and the Boston Symphony Orchestra have been invaluable in helping to develop a significant school of symphonic writing. In the course of time they all have turned out whole series of symphonies, written expressly for the Boston orchestra and generally introduced by Koussevitzky. Among the new compositions that the Boston programs record between 1931 and 1945 are three symphonies by Hill, four by Hanson, four by William Schuman, six by Roy Harris, and four Berezowsky symphonies.

Berezowsky's Second Symphony, Opus 18, dedicated to Koussevitzky, had its first performance from the manuscript score on

* The author has vivid recollection of this concerto's first performance, at Dresden on April 29, 1930, when Berezowsky conducted the Dresden Philharmonic Orchestra, and Carl Flesch, famous Berlin violinist and teacher, was the soloist. At the invitation of both Berezowsky and Flesch he made the trip from Berlin to Dresden expressly to hear the concerto and to make the acquaintance of the young Russian-American composer, at that time still entirely unknown. This trip proved to be worth while, and the author's favorable impressions are recorded in a report sent to the New York *Musical Courier* and published a few weeks later.

February 16, 1934. This work, as the composer tells us in the program book, is "not descriptive music in the literary sense. It is written in orthodox symphonic form with some modifications." One of these modifications, the absence of prescribed keys, indicates greater freedom of key relations and harmony in general than is practiced in fully orthodox scores. "The general mood of the first movement is lyric." The lively Scherzo has a trio written for brass and wood winds only. The Largo "begins in a very plaintive and tranquil manner, gradually rises to a more passionate mood and then ends quietly." A brief recapitulation of the principal theme of the first movement makes its appearance in this Largo. The finale "opens with a canon in four voices in a somewhat gay folk manner. . . . Fragmentary themes appear and reappear in lively fashion." Before the brilliant final climax the principal, first theme reappears, "but quickly fades away and gives place to a new theme" in the coda.

On February 22, 1935, Koussevitzky introduced Berezowsky's Concerto Lirico for Violoncello and Orchestra, which was played by the famous Russian cellist Gregor Piatigorsky, to whom it is dedicated. This concerto, in one movement, consists of a slow introduction to the principal theme of the work, which is conceived in the manner of a passacaglia, with five variations. Next there is a tarantella-like allegro, in which the passacaglia theme is incorporated. Following a brilliant climax is a cadenza by the solo instrument and a retrospective coda.

Berezowsky's Third Symphony, Opus 21, completed in 1936, had its first performance in January 1937 at Rochester, New York, with Jose Iturbi conducting. This speedy performance indicated that Berezowsky was already considered important enough for immediate action. The Boston performance followed on March 19, 1937, when the composer himself conducted his work. Koussevitzky must have been favorably impressed by the new score, for he conducted it himself on November 8, 1940. The analytic notes in the program book give a vague idea of the plan of construction but are too scant to help the memory in recalling the musical values of the symphony heard years ago. A first movement in orthodox sonata form plus a slow introduction is followed by a waltz-like second movement and a Lento, maestoso finale, in the manner of a theme with variations. A third performance on March 29, 1946, afforded a welcome opportunity to renew the acquaintance with a score that certainly does not charm the ear, but keeps the interest of a professional listener awake by its ingenious structure and the multitude of its ideas.

On October 21, 1938, Koussevitzky brought out for the first time Berezowsky's Toccata, Variations and Finale for String Quartet and Orchestra, Opus 23. The score is dedicated to Elizabeth Sprague Coolidge; and the Coolidge Quartet, of which Berezowsky had been a member for years, participated in this concert. One may best describe this unusual combination not as a modern concerto, but as a variant of the old concerto grosso, owing to the dialogue of the four solo instruments with the tutti of the orchestra. This dialogue, however, does not exclude a combination of both groups; the solo quartet weaves its melodic threads into the fabric of the tutti, not merely doubling the orchestral parts but maintaining within the ensemble its distinctive pattern of melody and rhythm. The score is interesting through its highly involved, yet clear, polyphony and through the statement of many unusual structural and formal problems.

After his violin and violoncello concertos heard at Boston, Berezowsky thought of the viola—the stepchild in the string family—and enriched the scant solo literature for this instrument with a new concerto, Opus 28, which Koussevitzky conducted on April 24, 1942. The structural plan of this concerto is unconventional, the composer's inventive power remarkable. This is a work demanding serious attention, but whether it will gain a permanent place in repertory can only be seen at some later time when a number of outstanding viola players have tested it. So far no viola concerto has been generally accepted, and it would be no small achievement for Berezowsky to have given the world the first one sufficiently interesting and attractive. The first three soloists have been the English viola virtuoso William Primrose; the composer himself; and, at Boston, Louis Bailly, viola player of the formerly world-famous Flonzaley Quartet.

The first movement of the viola concerto starts with a rhapsodic introduction and recitative, leading over to a theme with seven variations, and concluding with a cadenza over a pedal point. The theme is played by a trumpet, the solo instrument displaying its figuration with a plaintive accent quite in accord with the veiled tone of the viola. The second movement, Allegro rubato, makes use of this pronounced quality of the viola tone in a comic vein. A rustic dance tune of the solo instrument is accompanied by the queer combination of tuba, trombone, and triangle. Gradually, other instruments vary this somewhat burlesque episode. The third movement, Andante sostenuto, relies on the singing power, the alto character, of the viola, in a broad aria-like piece, accompanied by the string orchestra. The finale, Allegro commodo, con brio, is treated in the character of a rondo, speeding up toward the close.

Berezowsky's Fourth Symphony, Opus 29, was commissioned by the Koussevitzky Music Foundation, established in memory of Mme. Natalie Koussevitzky, the wife of Dr. Koussevitzky. Such a commission is a great honor, bestowed only on composers of recognized standing or of extraordinary promise. The new symphony had its initial performance on October 22, 1943, conducted by the composer. The score shows Berezowsky fully matured as a composer of serious symphonic music. His already well established style is continued here. Though this music is decidedly modern, Berezowsky had resisted the temptation of aiming at sensational novelty, usually purchased at the cost of pure style. The four movements, in the traditional symphonic forms, treat a plastic, characteristic, and arresting thematic material with considerable skill. Even after twenty years in America, during which time dozens of his works have been performed, Berezowsky has seen no reason to Americanize himself forcibly, preferring to follow his inborn musical instinct, to develop his individuality in a field with which he is thoroughly familiar. This tendency is to his credit as a creative artist. His Fourth Symphony means a wide step forward in the direction of a pronounced personal style.

Boris Koutzen, born in Southern Russia, 1901, was educated at the Moscow Conservatory and at Berlin as a violinist. He came to Philadelphia in 1923. A member of the Philadelphia Orchestra and later of the N.B.C. Orchestra in New York and head of the violin classes at the Philadelphia Conservatory, he aroused attention as a composer of orchestral and chamber music. On February 23, 1940, Koussevitzky performed Koutzen's Concerto for Five Solo Instruments and Orchestra. A quintet of flute, clarinet, bassoon, horn, and violoncello has the string orchestra as background. This work belongs to the species of the concerto grosso, an eighteenth-century form, revived in a modernized form by a considerable number of contemporary composers during the last twenty years. The three sections, Recitativo, Passacaglia, and Finale, all derive from the same thematic material. Many contrapuntal devices—basso ostinato, variation, inversion, combination of different themes—are exploited with skill, and the association of the solo quintet with the string orchestra gives rise to unusual sonorities that charm the ear.

Nicolai Lopatnikoff, born at Reval in Estonia, then a Russian province, in 1903, was a student at the famous St. Petersburg Conservatory until the Revolution expelled him to Finland. In 1920 he took up residence in Germany, at first in Karlsruhe, as a pupil of the eminent musician Ernst Toch, who is now teaching in California. A few years later he came to Berlin and was soon known as a highly gifted composer of the new, advanced school. A number of his works were heard at various festivals of modern music in Berlin and other cities. During this phase of his career he came to Koussevitzky's attention. On April 27, 1928, at Boston, Lopatnikoff's orchestral Scherzo, Opus 10, was performed for the first time anywhere.

Scarcely had Lopatnikoff arrived in New York in 1939, when he got in touch with Koussevitzky, and the speedy result of this contact was the first performance of Lopatnikoff's Second Symphony, Opus 24, in Boston on December 23, 1939. A young composer of remarkable stature was here introduced to America with a major work. His symphony does not, of course, reflect the new American tendencies but is interesting in that it shows the most advanced phase of European symphonic technique, in a compound of Russian, German, and French features of the late thirties. Worth attention is the composer's remark that his Second Symphony no longer reflects "the idiom and technique of atonality," to which some of his earlier works had been committed.

On April 17, 1942, Richard Burgin played for the first time Lopatnikoff's new Violin Concerto, Opus 26, a vigorous, bold work in the modern contrapuntal, linear style, revealing the composer's uncommon power of thematic invention as well as considerable constructive skill.

Lopatnikoff's Sinfonietta, Opus 28, was played in Boston on November 6, 1942, when Richard Burgin conducted. Already it had gained remarkable success at a League of Composers radio concert conducted by Howard Barlow, and at the Festival of the International Society for Contemporary Music held at the University of California. This sinfonietta is a typical but uncommonly competent sample of the neo-classic style of absolute music introduced by Hindemith and best represented in America by Walter Piston. It exemplifies the revival, with modern harmony and modern orchestration, of the old Bach concerto for orchestra. Lopatnikoff's orchestration also points to the methods of Stravinsky. The composer uses a full string orchestra as background on which the melodic phrases of only seven wind instruments—one of each kind—are projected. For fullness and rhythmic effects of percussion he uses a piano and kettle drums, tambourine, little drum, and cymbals. From this unconventional combination (only one horn, one trumpet, no trombones or tuba) he extracts all sorts of piquant and interesting sonorities and produces a fine transparency of the prevailing polyphonic structure. The spirited first movement in sonata form is followed by a thinly scored Andantino without percussion, in which the bassoon, oboe, clarinet, horn, and flute converse with each other in melodious phrases. The finale is a lively rondo in which piano and percussion instruments establish and maintain effective rhythmic energy.

The last work of Lopatnikoff heard at Boston was a Concertino for Orchestra, Opus 30, brought out by Koussevitzky for the first time on March 2, 1945. This score, commissioned by the Koussevitzky Foundation, is a fair sample of Lopatnikoff's energetic, finely proportioned, and organically constructed neoclassic style. Its three movements, Toccata, Elegietta, and Finale, develop their ideas tersely, with strong rhythmic drive, more intent on the contrapuntal linear play of their sharply profiled motives than on a display of color. In a work of this type Lopatnikoff's style is quite similar to Walter Piston's, with the difference that the one suggests, in a hardly definable manner, the Russian atmosphere, while the other contrives with about the same means to produce an American accent.

Arcady Dubensky (born in Russia in 1890) is at present a member of the first violin section of the New York Philharmonic–Symphony Orchestra. He has written a great many orchestral, chamber, and theatrical works, most of which reflect his youth spent in Russia. A few American themes, like the "Tom Sawyer" Overture (1935) or "Fantasy on a Negro Theme for Tuba and Orchestra" (1938), are among his works. He has been fond of unusual combinations like the tuba solo just mentioned, "Caprice for Piccolo and Orchestra," and the much-played "Fugue for Eighteen Violins" (1932). Koussevitzky performed Dubensky's well-written and impressive Prelude and Fugue for Orchestra, on April 12, 1943, and again on March 29, 1945. The prelude, Adagio, is written for string orchestra alone; the wind instruments and percussion instruments enter as the fugue is gradually expanded.

The Czech composer Bohuslav Martinu, for years a resident of America, was still studying and working in Paris when Koussevitzky first performed one of his scores, on November 18, 1927. Hearing the boisterous allegro, entitled "La Bagarre," one would hardly guess that its composer was a compatriot of Smetana and Dvořák. The fiery dance rhythms and melodious rustic tunes of classic Bohemian music are absent here, as well as the relationship to the German symphonic technique seen in the scores of Smetana and Dvořák. Instead Martinu's composition has a very modernistic touch, an unromantic, realistic energy, an unsentimental vitality, manifest in the unrelenting rhythmical force, in the regard for solid and logical construction rather than lyric emotionalism. The Parisian phase of Stravinsky profoundly influenced Martinu, as well as many of his most gifted contemporaries.

"La Bagarre" (approximately translated "tumult"), according to the composer's note in the Boston program, deals with the tension of spectators at a football game: "Chaos ruled by all the sentiments of enthusiasm, struggle, joy, sadness, wonder. . . . It is grandly contrapuntal . . . but not descriptive music." Here is found one of the earliest examples of sport as a subject for music. The program book listed the Boston performance of "La Bagarre" as the first one to be held anywhere. Yet at the International Festival in Prague, two years earlier, in May 1925, Martinu's "Half-time," also descriptive of a football game, had been performed. Perhaps "Half-time" and "La Bagarre" are identical, or the latter may be a revised version of the former piece, with a new title. In 1928 Honegger found inspiration in sport for his symphonic piece "Rugby," performed in Paris. Whether "La Bagarre" and "Rugby" are rival pieces, and which of the two is the earlier, are questions not answered from available sources.

"La Symphonie" by Martinu was performed for the first time by Koussevitzky on December 14, 1928. This score in one long movement is meant to commemorate an episode of the first World War: the presentation in June 1918 of a Czechoslovakian flag to a newly formed regiment of revolting Czech soldiers who were joining the Allies against Germany and Austria and thus helping the homeland to gain independence.

On December 22, 1932, another new Martinu composition appeared on a Boston program, a Piece for String Quartet with Orchestra.

More detailed information is available on the Martinu works heard in Boston during the forties. Martinu's Concerto Grosso had its first performance from manuscript on November 14, 1941, in Boston, and Koussevitzky repeated this interesting and successful work on January 2 of the same season. Though the score was ready in 1938 for performance in Paris and Prague and for publication by the Universal Edition in Vienna, these events failed to be realized, owing to the German invasion of Austria, Czechoslovakia, and in 1940 France. The composer lost his score on his hasty flight from Paris to America, but recovered it much later by a lucky chance. What distinguishes this concerto grosso from many others written in recent years is the use of two pianos, which the composer turns to best account. The score demands, besides the two pianos, only the string orchestra and the group of wood winds. The strictly polyphonic treatment of the entire concerto is particularly evident in the first movement, a brisk and strong Allegro. The second movement, Lento, is more lyric in character, a broad, serious, manly song that is mainly given to the strings. In the finale the two pianos as solo instruments are brilliantly displayed, partly by themselves, partly in coördination with the orchestra, as ornamental counterpoint in a lively and effective rondo.

Martinu's First Symphony, conducted by Koussevitzky, had its first public hearing on November 13, 1942. Although Martinu had never before written a symphony, he resolved to try his hand at one when he received a commission from the recently established Koussevitzky Foundation for a new symphonic score. In an extended exposition published in the Boston program book, he explained his ideas on the form and style of a modern symphony. These aesthetic discussions are of fundamental importance. For him the symphony is "a form well established not only in structure, but in its content of elevated expression and grandeur . . . a sentiment tragic, pathetic, even grandiloquent [has] placed the symphony at the highest level of musical composition." In this conservative outlook he does not agree with "attempts of contemporary composers to change the structure, to find another solution in writing a symphony in a single movement, in five parts, etc., its essential nature remains unchanged with rare exceptions." He goes on to explain that "The large proportions, the expansive form of the symphony necessarily force the composer to put himself on a high plane." As "elevated thought" is indispensable in a symphony, he asks what elevated thought really means, and comes to the conclusion that "thoughts and things which are quite simple . . . not explained in high-sounding words and abstruse phrases," may have an essential nobility and an "ethical and human significance." In other words, even simple things may "contain a deep meaning," may make life and art more enjoyable, and even "touch the highest plane of thought." Moreover one must recognize that a monumental work like Beethoven's Ninth Symphony could have been conceived and created "only at a certain moment in history with the concurrence of certain conditions, and could not have been written just by any one and just at any time." Not understanding this basic truth, composers may assume "a tragic and pathetic attitude, which would result in nothing else than a '*tour de force*.'" Martinu warns composers of "false magnitude" and maintains that intended tragedy and pathos may easily turn out to be not at all tragic. "Sentiments of grandeur and tragedy" are a great temptation to composers of our time. But "the desire to be greater than one is can lead directly to an emphasis which, to say the least, is not essentially musical."

He also points out a very common fault of modern orchestral music, overemphasis on sound and dynamics, or the "tendency to mask a lack of real music and to replace it with noise. The result adds nothing to the true beauty of the art, for the sheer excitation of the nerves cannot be the just aesthetic goal." He complains that this excess of dynamic power tends to make symphonic music "brass," while "the charm, the amiability, even the passion, of the stringed instruments and their great variety of expression" are lost. For him—contrary to the practice of Stravinsky and his school, who base orchestral writing on the wind instruments—"the basis of the orchestra is in the quintet of the strings." He stresses the importance of "measure," that is, moderation and right proportion, which he learned well in France. As to his symphony, Martinu states that he was not desirous of the "sonority of impressionism, nor is there the search for color, which rather is integral in the writing and the formal structure." The character of the symphony he calls calm and lyric.

Martinu's First Symphony, one of the most remarkable of

modern works, has been subjected to minute analysis by the author of this book, although only a brief condensation of this analysis can be given here. The first movement gives the impression of a powerful and intense symphonic requiem fantasy, mixing religious, profoundly sad, meditative traits with mystic, agitated, and ecstatic accents. The dedication, "To the Memory of Mrs. Natalie Koussevitzky," gives a clue to the composer's intention.

The second movement is a brilliant and fantastic Scherzo. Three tiny motives, the structural material of the entire piece, are shaken like dice, and continually produce interesting new combinations of sounds. As the mass of leaping, running, dancing tones is rapidly whirled around, melodic outlines are only vaguely defined and keep changing in details all the time. This piece is not built on definite themes but on the idea of an uninterrupted running and leaping, most capriciously and cleverly varied in accents. One might call the first part a capriccio fantasy on the scale motive. Then a gentler, more romantic, and lyric episode introduces coherent legato melody for the first time. The repetition of the first part is varied by what may be called "geometric" patterns—rhythmical, constantly recurring designs that suggest dots, straight or curved lines, triangular, square, circular, elliptic figures. Yet this apparently mechanical method is suggestive of great structural power and mental energy. To hear the musical precision-clockwork of this part is an exciting experience, for the accumulation of sound power is both dazzling and admirable. The trio, a very original and fascinating piece, is full of rare sonorities, owing to the exclusion of the strings and the fullest exploiting of the resources of all wind, brass, and percussion instruments. Two quite opposite features are here combined: a romantic, serenade-like love-song melody gets a complex accompaniment, of machine-like precision, this time gentle and refined.

The third movement, Largo, a solemn and austere piece, has a somber and mysterious introduction. Above a pedal point of tolling of bells, the violins unfold a broad melody of declamatory character, growing in intensity as it mounts higher and higher.

The grave simplicity, the darkly tinged color, and the pathos of this "eternal" melody remind one of a priest's sermon at a memorial service. Further on, the Catholic cathedral atmosphere is also suggested by the richly ornamented, dense net of arpeggios, tremoli, staccato scales, and legato passages, through which the plain melody shows forth somewhat dimmed and weakened. Over organlike sustained chords of the brass, the ornamental design gradually disappears with a soft whispering of strings pizzicati and delicate harp and piano figuration. In the second part a magnificent climax is built up on the saraband rhythm that dominates the greater part of the piece, emphasizing still more the solemn archaic impression. In the coda, bare saraband chords again get a fanciful veil of chromatic scales in parallel fourths and seconds and in canonic imitation; this adds strange, mysterious, indefinable dissonances and swiftly passing disharmonic friction to the plain chords. The deeply impressive piece closes in a solemn and beautiful pianissimo.

The finale, a widely expanded Rondo, is in its musical substance more popular than the other movements, despite elaborate treatment of the thematic material, which approaches Slavic folksongs and dance rhythms. These arabesques are like flower wreaths and brilliant jewelry superimposed on the main melody and do not generally acquire the melodic status of really polyphonic countermelodies. The principal theme, pianissimo, is like march music heard from a distance, and in many variants the martial rhythm pervades the piece. It is interrupted by a litany phrase that is reminiscent of a church procession. Other episodes exhale an almost Brucknerian Catholic romanticism at the central climax, in which the *Dies irae* theme of the first movement reappears. These ecclesiastic sections are relieved by an outburst of energy and vivacity of a very worldly character, with march rhythms. There follow several alternations of these contrasting religious and secular episodes, culminating in a hymnlike, vigorous, and majestic peroration that soars higher and higher.

Martinu's First Symphony shows a change of style. His former works are finished examples of neo-classical constructivism with its strictly contrapuntal, unromantic attitude. The First Symphony, however, returns to a romantic, highly emotional expressiveness and makes ample use of ornamental design, thus mixing neo-classical with picturesque traits in a way reminiscent of impressionism.

A new work of Martinu, a Violin Concerto, had its first public hearing in Koussevitzky's concert on December 31, 1943. This remarkable score came into existence at the request of the eminent violinist Mischa Elman, who had been greatly impressed by Martinu's symphony and wanted to play a concerto written expressly for him by Martinu. The remarks of the composer on the new composition as well as on the problem of a modern violin concerto in general are so valuable that one would be tempted to quote them extensively if space permitted. Martinu calls the writing of a violin concerto a "most difficult problem," as the violin solo requires a quite special "state of mind." "For the violin solo, all which we wish to express must be contained in a single line, which must also imply the rest . . . the single part of the violin solo must in itself already contain the whole musical scheme, the whole concerto." But, as Martinu points out, "In working with the orchestra, we have lost the capacity of 'thinking solo.' " The modern composer, skilled in handling the orchestra, is tempted to express something essentially orchestral even in connection with a solo violin. He is apt to intensify the power of tone. "The dynamics, nuances, and the difference between $p-mf-f$ of the violin solo are limited and in no way comparable to the dynamic power of the string orchestra. In short, we confound a single violin with a group of violins, with a resulting conflict between desire and ability. It is just here that a composition requires a different state of mind for its whole structure and for the content of the musical idea." Experience shows that just at this point composers fail. Martinu's Violin Concerto is evidently the outcome of these and similar reasonings.

Modestly Martinu remarked that he did not claim to have fully solved the problem of writing a violin concerto, and how far he has succeeded can only be answered by experience with his new score. But even now it may be asserted that he attacked the problem in an original and masterly manner. The solo violin properly dominates the composition; and the orchestra, while mainly supporting the solo, is by no means insignificant, and adds charming, bright touches and interesting side remarks. The work starts with a broadly sung Andante, a noble lyric strain. It passes over into a brilliant Allegro section, where the virtuoso is allowed to shine for a while before the first andante theme claims its rights again, closing the movement, not without giving the soloist another chance with an elaborate cadenza. The second movement is a quiet intermezzo, lightly accompanied by the orchestra. The vigorous finale immediately follows the intermezzo; the soloist is leading most of the time; the orchestra replies occasionally in firm, massive, tutti sections. Mischa Elman's playing, masterly in every respect, presented to the listener whatever charm, beauty, and ingenuity is contained in Martinu's music.

The fascination of the violin concerto problem is revealed in the fact that during the last fifteen years no less than fourteen new violin concertos have been heard in the Boston Symphony concerts: by Achron, Berezowski, Hill, Dukelsky, Piston, Carpenter, Lopatnikoff, Bloch, Barber, Bartók, Stravinsky, Hindemith, and Martinu, to which list Gruenberg's concerto might be added, though not yet heard in Boston. Whether any of these works will pass over into permanent violin repertory remains to be seen. The Sibelius, Glazounoff, and second Prokofieff violin concertos have been the only fairly successful ones written since 1900.

Like his Concerto Grosso, Martinu's Double Concerto was a work for two pianos. It was played by Pierre Luboschutz and Genia Nemenoff at Koussevitzky's concert on October 20, 1944. Here, as in the Violin Concerto, Martinu's former strict neoclassical style is considerably modified. Brilliant ornamental passages, arpeggios, and virtuoso display, avoided by the modern neoclassic school, make their return in this representative work of a leading modernist. The composer himself explains that he saw fit to use the two pianos "in the purely solo sense," and the orchestra for mere accompaniment. His score "demands virtuosity, brilliant piano technique"; moreover "the timbre of the same two instruments calls forth new colors and new sonorities." This pianistic virtuosity is made to vie with Martinu's contrapuntal virtuosity in a novel-sounding and interesting contest, especially in the brisk first movement, "as the pianists weave into the pattern a texture of sixteenth-note figures, or shifting arpeggios." In the slow movement the two pianos intimately converse with each other; the orchestra throws in sporadic remarks and for a while dominates the scene, then retires and listens to the dialogue of the two solo instruments. The finale is a vivid and gay Rondo, coming closer to popular Bohemian tunes than is usual in Martinu's music. It is worth noticing that the rondo form, little used in romantic music, is revived in many modern works because of its playful vivacity, which accords with the recent stylistic trend.

Martinu's Third Symphony, heard for the first time on October 12, 13, 1945, is certainly worthy of the respect due to a master who has proved his artistic worth a dozen times or more. This new score is dedicated "To Serge Koussevitzky and the Boston Symphony Orchestra" on the occasion of Koussevitzky's twentieth anniversary as conductor of the Boston orchestra, in 1944. It is a tribute of thanks for invaluable services to the composer. The three movements of the Third Symphony respond again to the aesthetic creed of faith proclaimed by Martinu on the occasion of his First Symphony and partly quoted above. In their musical substance and in their symphonic structure they appear simpler and less pretentious than the First Symphony. Generally in a lighter vein than its predecessor, this younger score has a brighter, friendlier aspect and is more easily accessible. For these reasons it may easily be underrated.

A few composers who do not seem to fit into any group described in this book may find their place here.

The only appearance on the long list of Boston programs of the name Timothy Mather Spelman was in the season 1925–1926, when Koussevitzky conducted that composer's tone-poem

"Assisi, the Great Pardon of Saint Francis." This is one part of a series of four orchestral pieces entitled "Saints' Days," all concerned with legends of the Catholic Church. Philip Hale's program notes state that Spelman was born in Brooklyn in 1891 and received his musical education at Harvard and in Munich. For about fifteen years his name has hardly ever appeared on American symphonic programs. Yet Spelman has written and published a number of symphonic works, an opera, and some chamber music, and up to 1925 his works were heard not only in New York, Boston, and Chicago but also in London and Paris. One gets the impression that this American composer made a promising start twenty years ago but was checked in his career.

During his lifetime Hermann Hans Wetzler was better known in Germany than in America, though he resided for several periods in the United States. Born in 1870 in Frankfurt, Germany, the son of American parents, he spent his early youth in America, then returned to Germany for a musical education. Back in America again, he was active for a dozen years in New York as an organist, orchestral player, and conductor. Later he became an opera conductor in a number of German opera houses and acquired considerable reputation as a composer. His orchestral legend "Assisi," Opus 13, made the rounds of German concert halls and won a thousand-dollar prize in Chicago. His opera *Die baskische Venus,* first performed in Leipzig in 1928, was much remarked, and its ballet music was heard in many German concert halls. Called "Symphonic Dance in Basque Style," it came to Boston Symphony Hall on November 29, 1929, and was repeated on February 28, 1936, both times conducted by Richard Burgin. This suite of four Basque dances, Fandango, Zortziko, Espatadantza, Arin-Arin, is brilliantly written, for Wetzler, a master of the modern orchestra, has acquired intimate acquaintance with the peculiar melodic, rhythmic, and dynamic features of the racy Basque dances. Wetzler in these pieces rivals Ravel, a similar connoisseur of Basque music.

Jakobus Langendoen is another composer from the ranks of the Boston Symphony, as were Loeffler, Strube, and Eichheim before him. This unusual number of composers within its membership speaks eloquently for the superior musicianly qualities of the Orchestra. A Dutch musician, Langendoen was educated in Holland and in Berlin, and has been a violoncellist with the Orchestra since 1920. On March 4, 1927, Koussevitzky performed his "Variations on a Dutch Theme of Adrianus Valerius" for string orchestra. The composer took as his theme the famous Netherlandish song "Bergen-op-Zoom," written on the liberation of the city of Bergen from the Spanish siege in 1622. The Boston program is in error in ascribing the tune to Adrianus Valerius, who was not the composer but the author of the text and the editor of the collection in which the song was published.

Langendoen's name appears for a second time on January 20, 1939, when his "Improvisations for Orchestra" were first performed in America, in a concert conducted by Richard Burgin. Formerly the work had been played several times in Holland. This suite of four pieces entitled "Unisono—Capriccio—Pastorale and Procession—Burleska" shows the skilful hand of a composer thoroughly familiar with orchestral technique and well versed in problems of musical structure and thematic development.

For a single time the name of Allan Arthur Wilman occurs in the Boston programs, when Koussevitzky on April 20, 1936, performed for the first time this composer's symphonic poem "Solitude." Wilman, a young composer from Illinois (b. 1909), educated at Chicago, was hardly known in the East before the "Solitude" score earned him the Paderewski Prize of one thousand dollars, awarded by a jury consisting of Edward B. Hill, Sigismund Stojowsky (a former pupil of Paderewski), and Deems Taylor.

Gian Carlo Menotti, Italian-born composer, now thirty-five years of age, had the unique good fortune of finding the New York Metropolitan Opera inclined to produce not only one, but even two of his operatic works. For the first time some of his music was heard in Boston, when Koussevitzky performed on October 19 and 20, 1945, two orchestral interludes from Menotti's opera "The Island God." These well-sounding, colorful pieces appeared somewhat empty in musical substance at

Symphony Hall. Accompanying scenic pictures in the opera house they probably served their purpose better than isolated as absolute music. A fortnight later, on November 2 and 3, another Menotti score was heard, when the brilliant Czech pianist Rudolf Firkusny played for the first time Menotti's Piano Concerto in F major. This is not great or eminent, but agreeable and entertaining music, very Italian in character and sentiment. Its agility, grace, and limpidity derived from Domenico Scarlatti's art, are certainly commendable features.

In the mid twenties the author of this book was called upon to introduce Henry Cowell at a concert in Berlin, given by the lately founded International Society for Contemporary Music. At that time Cowell was, in Europe, considered the only American representative of musical modernism, and his "tone clusters," hit with the fist or the fore-arm on the piano keys, his harp-playing on the strings of the piano, were sensational features. His symphonic poem "Synchrony" was included in the programs of ultra-modern American music conducted by Nicolas Slonimsky in Paris in 1931, and by Stokowski in Philadelphia in 1932. As time advanced, younger competitors in modernism eclipsed Cowell's place in the front rank. Yet he did modernism a great service by his publication of a long series of "New Music," including many radical works which elsewhere had no chance of publication at all. The Boston Symphony programs have ignored Cowell's music persistently, with the solitary exception of his "Hymn and Fuguing Tune" that reached Boston Symphony Hall rather late, on March 29 and 30, 1946. This score is miles distant from the efforts of our younger modernists. It looks not into the future but back into the past, taking up again the quaint style of that strange amateur-musician of eighteenth-century Boston, William Billings, whose primitive but expressive use of ecclesiastic "fuguing tunes" has only recently been revived to a certain extent. Needless to state, this Cowell score is in point of dissonance and progressive devices the mildest one of all the many modern works heard at Boston. Yet it is not devoid of a certain old-fashioned charm and flavor.

CHAPTER 10

THE NEO–CLASSICISM OF
STRAVINSKY AND HINDEMITH
IN AMERICAN MUSIC

After the impressionist wave had lost much of its impact on the American shore, and after the extravagant Americanism of jazz, programmatic music, and fantastic tone pictures had spent much of its force, new influences of a neo-classical nature began to assert themselves. This took place about 1930, and the two leaders of the new musical creed were Stravinsky and Hindemith. Both have settled in the United States, and by their works as well as by their teaching they have deeply impressed the younger generation of American composers.* Stravinsky has lectured at Harvard University, and Hindemith is a permanent member of the Yale faculty. Even before they took up residence in America both masters had been widely known in this country by their constantly performed works. Stravinsky has, from his Russian start, gradually drifted over into a frankly international course, whereas Hindemith, in the thirties generally acknowledged as the leader of the new German music, has preserved much more of his Germanic basis.

As early as the twenties the numerous American pupils of Nadia Boulanger in Paris had been initiated by her into the Stravinsky cult, since she was one of its enthusiastic propagandists. Upon returning to America, these students brought with them their newly acquired taste for the severe—even ascetic—unsentimental, and unadorned constructivism of Stravinsky's

* It is surprising how little recent American music has been affected by the real father of modern music, Arnold Schönberg. Since 1933 he has been a resident of America, and he is a famous teacher, a world-renowned though not widely understood composer, and the acknowledged head of the modern international movement. Even so, he has not yet impressed his seal perceptibly on the new American music.

Parisian phase. Specifically, it was a phase that eliminated pictorial associations, laid stress on logical development, contrapuntal virtuosity, and rhythm as dominant forces, and revived such eighteenth-century forms as the fugue, canon, partita, passacaglia, and concerto grosso.

This new, absolute music is on its surface not much touched by American tendencies. It rather aims at an up-to-date internationalism, and only after close inspection and considerable familiarity with it can one detect certain American features, which have crept in slyly and are seemingly unintended, even unnoticed, by the composers.

The American neo-classical school is represented in its strictest observance by Roger Sessions and especially by Walter Piston. Other leaders of this new American music are Aaron Copland, Roy Harris, and William Schuman, but they do not confine themselves so closely to the well-defined laws of the new style. Their art, as will be shown later, adds to the neo-classic substance various other ingredients, notably a stronger accent on Americanism.

On April 22, 1927, the name of Roger Sessions made its first appearance on a Koussevitzky program, with a Symphony in E minor. Like the debut of Aaron Copland, this was a first performance of a little-known composer's recent work. Evidently after his discovery of Copland, Koussevitzky was looking for a second young American of great promise; but in Sessions' case he must have been disappointed, for he has never performed another of his works. This may seem strange to some observers, since Sessions' colleagues among the progressive younger American composers have authorized him to be the spokesman for their common aims and interests. He has been sent as American delegate to several congresses of the International Society for Contemporary Music, which has included some of his works on its international programs. Moreover, Sessions has written a number of weighty essays in which the philosophy of the new American music is explained and analyzed. His philosophical and aesthetic tendencies led him to make some remarkable statements in the Boston program book on the occasion when his symphony was performed. Among other things, he acknowledged his debt of gratitude to Ernest Bloch, with whom he had studied. He also pointed to the strong influences on his music exerted by Bloch and Stravinsky. But one looks in vain in the program book for any specific information on the style and contents of his symphony.

There is some difficulty at the present time in acquiring a close acquaintance with Sessions' major works, as very few of his compositions are available in print, and performances have been infrequent during the past few years. It would be interesting to compare the critical comments of the Boston press after the performance of the Symphony in E minor with what the European critics had to say when the same symphony was played at the International Festival in Geneva, April 1929, were it possible to collect these European articles of twenty years ago.

Walter Piston made his first appearance on a Boston Symphony program on March 23, 1928, with a "Symphonic Piece." Educated at Harvard and one of the first American pupils of Nadia Boulanger, he returned from Paris to Harvard as an instructor in the music department, where he now holds a professorship. Altogether Piston's name has occurred in Boston Symphony programs no less than eleven times, with a number of scores. From the start, his music stressed strict polyphony in a modern style. Stravinsky's neo-classicism as well as Hindemith's contrapuntal mastery have left distinct traces in Piston's music without obliterating his personal traits. Structural problems at first meant more to him than did melodic distinction, but as time progressed the severity of his style has mellowed and given way to stretches of singing melody, shining through a tightly woven yet transparent contrapuntal web.

One can roughly divide all of Piston's orchestral music into two types, which for the sake of brevity may be called the suite and the concerto type. In the suite-like works the strictly linear, severe contrapuntal style of the concertos is mixed with outbursts of orchestral extravagance, full of colorful sound effects. The concerto-like pieces, though more austere, have plenty of vigorous motion in all parts, as plastic, rhythmically solid motives are

tossed about in different parts; moreover, there is animated con-
versation among these motives. All these points are strongly
reminiscent of a Bach concerto. The resulting harmony in the
modern piece, however, is spiced with many so-called dissonant
notes which prevent intentionally the clear-cut tonality characteristic of Bach and produce an acrid sound, a kaleidoscopic,
quick and frequent change of only partially defined tonalities,
a new nervous irritability that is different from the romantic
upheaval of sentiment. This harmony of Piston's is not identical
with what is commonly called the atonality of Schönberg nor
with the systematic polytonality practiced by some modern
Frenchmen.

In notes written for the program book Piston is usually very
sparing with comments on his intentions and on the character
and contents of his music. The absence of pictures, of suggestive
descriptions in many of his scores means that his music goes
unadorned before the listener; accordingly, Piston believes that
whatever there is in the music will be noticed by the listener and
requires no roundabout explanations. This philosophy is the
basis of so-called "absolute music" of the purest type, and there
is really nothing to be said against it. The only difficulty is that
such highly involved music needs a highly trained listener fully
to appreciate its merits.

With regard to the Suite for Orchestra, performed for the first
time on March 28, 1930, Piston was unusually communicative.
He stated that "the first movement is light in character and contains some 'Americanism'; but it is in no sense an attempt to
write jazz. The second movement is calm, and is a development
of two motives, one announced by the violas, the other by the
English horn. The third movement is a fugue." After this modest
and brief description one might expect to hear a piece in
chamber-music manner for a few instruments; instead, the score
demands a large modern orchestra with pianoforte, wood block,
and a whole battery of percussion instruments. Here Piston
follows the trail marked by Stravinsky in "Petrouchka." The
austere linear counterpoint, with its pencil strokes in a black
and white design, is mixed with a colorful orchestral treatment

that is not devoid of picturesque suggestiveness, within the limits of a strictly organic, thematic structure. A few steps further in that direction led Piston to a more outspoken and characteristic picturesqueness in his interesting ballet music "The Incredible Flutist," performed years later by Arthur Fiedler at a Boston Pops Concert.

As his third work written for the Boston Orchestra, Piston presented his new Concerto for Orchestra at a concert in Sanders Theatre, Cambridge, March 4, 1934. It was repeated in Boston on March 29. Both times he himself conducted. The work must have impressed Koussevitzky, for he put it on the program of the first Berkshire Festival, August 5, 1939, this time conducting it himself. The line indicated in Piston's earlier compositions is here followed consistently. Again he is interested in constructive problems and in a logical, polyphonic presentation of his ideas. The old form of the concerto grosso, as practiced by Bach and Handel, is here employed in a modern manner. The traditional division into tutti (the full orchestra) and concertino (a little group of solo instruments) is maintained. Yet in the interest of a more colorful sound effect, Piston does not confine the concertino group to the same ensemble of instruments throughout the piece but makes use of a different combination every time the group appears. The second movement has a scherzo character and is developed with considerable contrapuntal elaboration. In the last section the contrapuntal devices of imitation and inversion in retrograde motion are exploited. The finale adapts the structural idea of the old passacaglia to the resources of the large modern orchestra. Again contrapuntal features like fugato, ostinato figures, stretto imitation, and canon are applied with much skill and ingenuity, resulting in a piece that combines modern wealth of tonal color with an intricate, interesting construction. One of the best works of its type, this concerto is among the few modern American orchestral compositions available in a printed edition.

When Piston's Concerto was performed in New York in February 1936, Olin Downes in the *New York Times* commented on this "brilliantly composed concerto." He called it "music ex-

tremely well written, and this with exceptional spirit and invention in the modern metamorphosis of the old classic form." He
singles out Piston as "the still exceptional figure among native
composers: a young man who in the first place has thoroughly
mastered the ground principles of his art; who knows what he
wants to do and how to do it; whose basis is a thorough command of counterpoint and form, on which is superimposed brilliant treatment of the orchestra." In the same article, Mr. Downes
paid tribute to "Dr. Koussevitzky's originality and enterprise in
program making, to his rare gifts as an interpreter, and to the
qualities of the wonderful orchestra . . . endowed with a sensi-
bility and a tone quality that would set the famous band apart
from any other, whenever or wherever it played." He spoke
further of the "incalculable aid that Dr. Koussevitzky has given
the rising generation of American composers. He . . . met talent
with the understanding and sympathy so badly needed . . . he
has not played new music simply because it was new; he has
been quick to recognize merit, and thus has added a very considerable number of worthwhile native compositions to the
orchestral repertory."

On April 8, 1938, Piston brought out his First Symphony, conducting it himself. Though called a symphony, this score might
just as well have been entitled a concerto, and conversely, Piston's
older concerto for orchestra might be termed a symphony. The
style in the two works is not greatly differentiated. In the symphony one finds the contrapuntal texture of the concerto, the
same terse statement of themes, the intricate interweaving of
melodic lines, the frequent clash of acrid harmony resulting from
the logical progression of several melodies meeting at a certain
point. The listener is not charmed by any outpouring of singing
melody, for this severe music turns its back on lyric effusions in
the romantic tradition. But though lacking sweetness it has its
own tang and zest, manly energy, and rhythmic vitality. The symphony begins with a slow introduction, presenting the thematic
germs from which the entire work grows. The Allegro of the
first movement modifies the sonata form as it tends towards
brevity, omits rhetoric ornament, and suddenly closes without

the customary coda. The second movement, Adagio, is written in the almost indispensable three-part form with intermezzo, following the formula A B A. The vigorous finale merges features of the rondo and variation forms in an ingenious and interesting manner. The powerful close rounds off the carefully planned structure with a magnified repetition of the slow introduction, the meaning of which is only now fully disclosed.

In 1937 the Columbia Broadcasting System commissioned a number of prominent American composers to write new works especially designed for radio performance. Walter Piston's Concertino for Piano and Chamber Orchestra was one of these new scores, and it was repeatedly broadcast in 1937 with Sanromá as soloist and Howard Barlow as conductor. In February 1938, Bernard Zighera conducted the work at its first concert performance, with his chamber group of Boston Symphony Orchestra players; and on November 10, 1939, Koussevitzky presented the score in Symphony Hall. The Piston Concertino is one of the few modern American works available in print and can therefore be studied at leisure. Those in quest of outspoken Americanism will find little to satisfy their craving in this concertino, as indeed in all of Piston's music so far. In fact, were these works performed anonymously at an international festival it would be unlikely that they could be easily identified as American. One needs a very close acquaintance with the American character in order to find certain American traits in the straightforward energy, the rhythmical vigor, the veiling of sentiment in Piston's music. All these positive as well as negative qualities are found in the Concertino, one of Piston's most representative and mature works.

In his conception of "Americanism" Piston agrees with the view of Howard Hanson, reported elsewhere in this book (p. 41). Piston, one learns from the Boston program book of January 31, 1941, does not advocate deliberate efforts at Americanism in music but prefers a gradual, quiet, and continuous growth. An American school, he wrote, "will be built by those men, living in America, knowing it and partaking of it, who are true to themselves. . . . If the composers will increasingly strive to perfect themselves in the art of music and will follow only those paths of expression which seem to them the true way, the matter of a national school will take care of itself." Such an attitude is perfectly natural and legitimate for an artist of Piston's peculiar mentality and temperament. But there are many diverging mentalities and temperaments in America, and others will look for more direct approaches, more clearly defined and specialized purposes in their quest of a national American music.

Written as one continuous, rather extended piece, the Concertino is subdivided into five sections that correspond to the single movements of a sonata. The principal theme—or more precisely, the fundamental motive—is plastic, rhythmically sharp, vigorous, easily retained in the memory. These qualities make it suitable as a principal motive to be subjected to many variants and developments in the course of the piece. The first, energetic statement is followed in effective contrast by a more lyrical variant of the same theme in cantabile manner—longer notes, in augmentation, played by the piano, legato and espressivo. The staccato and marcato prevailing in the beginning section return soon after the lyric intermezzo and serve as transition to the second section, in which the principal motive is transformed into a sprightly scherzo. In the midst of it the quintet of wood winds inserts a densely interwoven fugato, after which the light and lively scherzando in 6/8 time is expanded again in the piano part, after a while vanishing as the rhythms get broader, leading over to the central section, an adagio in 5/4 time. Here the principal part is allotted to a violoncello solo that sings a new, broad melody of almost romantic sentiment. The piano accompanies softly, throwing a colorful veil in Debussy style over the string orchestra, exploiting the sonorities of the low, medium, and high octaves of the instrument. The severity of the black and white linear style prevailing in Piston's music is here softened by a touch of colorful romantic impressionism. All the wind instruments in solo or duet episodes, the piano solo, and the string quintet discourse on the cantabile theme in a truly—to use an old-fashioned term—beautiful manner. This lyric section is, however, not allowed to languish in softness and sweetness. The piano solo cuts off such inclinations with a crescendo, rubato, stringendo episode, restoring the dominant martellato sound and terminating in a brilliant cadenza of the solo instrument. Here the virtuoso, so far restrained, is let loose in traditional concerto manner, but not before he pays tribute to the modern style with a thematic derivation from the adagio theme, plus canonic treatment. Next follows a variation of the first section, in classical reprise style and with a brilliant coda having thematic allusions. The orchestral part maintains a conspicuous economy of means, all the time in polyphonic intercourse with a minimum of massive tutti.

Piston wrote his Violin Concerto expressly for Ruth Posselt, an able and indefatigable promoter of modern violin concertos. On March 18, 1940, she played the new work for the first time, in Carnegie Hall, New York, at a concert of the National Orchestral Association, Leon Barzin conducting. Koussevitzky included the Piston Concerto on his program of January 31, 1941, and again Ruth Posselt was soloist. The three movements in elaborate symphonic structure are not of a type to invite the enthusiastic applause of the average Symphony Hall audience. The solo part is neither alluring through sheer beauty of sound nor dazzling in brilliance. Yet the musical substance and the workmanship are of a high order. As a sample of the structural complication of the score, the composer's formal analysis in the Boston program book of the concerto's Rondo-Finale in D major is reproduced here:

Theme I in solo violin after short introduction.
Theme II is a rhythmic transformation of the second theme of the first movement.
Theme III in canon—horn and solo violin—over staccato accompaniment.
Cadenza, combining Themes II and III, before the coda.
Form A B A C A B A, cadenza, coda.

This (A B A, etc.) refers to the reappearance, four times, of the principal theme in the Rondo form.

Piston's Sinfonietta was heard for the first time in Boston at Bernard Zighera's Chamber Orchestra concert, and later, on January 30, 1942, was conducted by Richard Burgin at Symphony

Hall. The work, in three movements, represents Piston's art in its full maturity and mastery of form and contents. On a smaller scale, with a modest array of orchestral means, the Sinfonietta is a younger sister of the full-grown Second Symphony, being less powerful, less stirring emotionally, less rich in dramatic accent and color, but full of slender grace and captivating with its beautiful curving outline. Couples of flutes, oboes, clarinets, bassoons, and horns, plus the string orchestra are the only instruments used—no trumpets, trombones, or percussion instruments being required. This score is the modern equivalent not of a Mozart or Haydn symphony but of a serenade or cassatio by those masters.

The Sinfonietta's first movement, Allegro grazioso, in well-defined E minor, is content with but two themes: the first a soft, elegiac melody, dolce, sung by the violins, which gathers force and breadth as it proceeds; the second a rhythmically more pointed theme, of sharper profile, marchlike, and set forth by the wood-wind group before the strings take over and lead to the culmination. The development section is like chamber music in that it has transparency and delicacy in the melodic lines—thin threads, piano and pianissimo, with more rests than notes. Strictly thematic, this section nevertheless contrives to introduce melodic surprises in a romantic horn solo, dolcissimo and espressivo, evolved from the principal theme. In the second part of this section Piston built up a brilliant climax from motives of the first theme, the music then descending step by step from its brief fortissimo to piano, and back to the elegiac first theme. The recapitulation of the entire first part, demanded by the sonata form of the piece, is ingeniously varied, and as the climax of the entire movement occurs the marchlike second theme is heard again. From this forceful and brilliant tutti there follows a constant decline in a coda, vanishing to pianissimo, with the plaintive first theme sung by the pale and fragile flute.

The second movement, Adagio, is filled with a kind of eternal melody, sad, interspersed with gentle sighs, momentarily raising its voice to an outburst of longing only to return to its intimate sentiment with piano and pianissimo phrases. A single broadly expanded theme dominates the piece; its phrases are sung successively by the oboe, horn, violins, flute, oboe, and other instruments in little monologues, here and there expanded into duets and dialogues against a soft, darkly tinged, subdued background. This noble piece might best be classified as a cavatina, of which the most exalted model is found in Beethoven's String Quartet, Opus 130.

The finale, Allegro vivo, is all bustle and energy. Stamping, shouting, running, and jumping fill the first part, where a rapid motive in 6/8 time is expanded with vigor and brilliance. After a while a piano episode brings effective contrast. A second, quiet theme enters dolce cantando, legato, played by the violoncellos, taken up by the violins. Here the 6/8 figure creeps in again, as a counterpoint in flutes and clarinets. At first this 6/8 is in smooth legato, but it soon resumes its original staccato, leading to a free reprise of the first section. A second piano episode exploits the singing second theme against the running and jumping motive. In rondo style the first theme returns again, forte, followed by a new episode, a fugato on the principal motive, with new, vigorous, running counterpoints. Here the culmination is reached, shortly before the brilliant, intentionally abrupt close.

Piston's Second Symphony was heard at Boston Symphony Hall in a concert conducted by G. Wallace Woodworth, the conductor of the Harvard Glee Club, on April 6, 1944. This symphony also has three movements—the structural plan always adhered to by Piston in his sinfoniettas, concertos, and suites. In fact this symphony, without a scherzo, does not differ considerably in form and style from Piston's orchestral concertos. Martinu's demand for "elevated expression and grandeur" in a symphony is only partially heeded by Piston. He evidently does not care much for grandeur but is much occupied in this score with elevated expression. In this latter respect, in fact, one may consider Piston's Second Symphony to have surpassed all other works that he had thus far produced. His melodic invention is here animated by a greater warmth and emotional intensity than is found in his earlier works. At the same time the severity and complexity of his contrapuntal writing is softened and simplified; nevertheless,

Piston retains his former mastery of polyphonic treatment, plus an admirable transparency in the now less tightly woven contrapuntal texture. These features of the composer's fully mature and somewhat mellow art are especially patent in the Adagio, the second movement—which fully deserves the epithet "beautiful," rarely if ever applicable to earlier Piston works. Here, as stated in the composer's own words, is "a quiet and lyric development," a novel feature in contrast with the brisk motion and the avoidance of lyric, romantic sentiment for which Piston formerly had little predilection. Gradually romanticism is seen furtively reëntering the domains of modern music, from which it had been strictly excluded for a time.

The Second Symphony's first movement, now a Moderato instead of the usual Allegro, is also based on a "flowing theme" of melodious, legato nature; and the rhythmically sharp, staccato motion formerly favored by Piston is now relegated to the background, as an effectively contrasting counterpoint to the softer principal theme. Likewise the pianissimo close of the first movement discloses a new attitude. In the brilliant third movement, the vigorous, rhythmic first theme and the marchlike second theme maintain the bustling vivacity, seasoned with a savory discordant harmony, appropriate to a symphonic finale. Yet care is taken here to temper the prevalent harshness of sound with a lyric third theme, in which the English horn and the clarinet display their singing voices. In all respects, Piston's Second Symphony is one of the few really distinguished, most highly accomplished symphonic scores so far written in America. After a performance in New York, conducted by Howard Hanson in May 1945, the circle of New York critics singled out Piston's Second Symphony as the most remarkable new American symphonic work of the season 1944–1945. One is justified in attributing to this score a fair chance for longer survival than is the lot of most of the ambitious novelties heard in our concerts.

A smaller work by Piston, Prelude and Allegro for Organ and Strings, was heard at Symphony Hall on October 29, 1943, and was repeated by Koussevitzky on April 20, 1945. The piece was originally written for the series of Sunday morning recitals on the baroque organ of the Harvard Germanic Museum. E. Power Biggs, the distinguished organist of the Boston Symphony Orchestra, who had played the piece in Cambridge, also performed it at both Koussevitzky's concerts. As one might have expected, Piston's contrapuntal mastery is turned to best account in this short organ composition. Canon, variation, and toccata elements enliven the organic development of the melodic thematic material, entrusted mainly to the strings. Yet these contrapuntal features are only of secondary importance in a piece more akin to a Handel organ concerto than to a prelude and fugue by Bach. The prelude is a discourse of the organ and the string band on gently flowing, roundly curved, melodious phrases in smooth legato. The Allegro is full of vivid, brilliant, running passages, in homophonic manner, reminiscent of a Handel finale. The orchestra responds in effective contrast with vigorous fugato sections, calling forth an animated "concerto"; there is, so to speak, a contest of the organ with the strings, in which both variation and toccata technique are displayed to best advantage. This grateful and effective work revives a type of organ music lately neglected, the type of the formerly famous Rheinberger organ concertos, which themselves derive from Mendelssohn's organ sonatas and Handel's concertos.

CHAPTER 11

THE NEW AMERICANISM OF
THE THIRTIES AND FORTIES

Of all American composers of the present time, no one has been more discussed than Aaron Copland. In Chapter 2 the discovery of him by Koussevitzky and the young musician's debut in 1925 have been described. Copland, an agile and active composer, and one who is more versatile than any of his American competitors, does not identify himself with any single predominant style. Though strongly influenced by Stravinsky's neo-classicism and acrid harmony, he does not follow the Stravinsky road to its ultimate limits. He jumps over the fence, so to speak, into the field of American popular music, pays his tribute to jazz, to radio and motion picture music, to Broadway theatrical shows, to ballet, and mixes in an occasional piece of serious nature and elevated contents.

After the violent clash of opinions provoked by Copland's Symphony for Organ and Orchestra in February 1925, Koussevitzky waited nine months before he put another sample of American modernism on his program. Then, on November 20 of that year, he introduced Copland's "Music for the Theatre," which had been completed two months previously, and which was dedicated to Koussevitzky. The title of the score has a broad meaning and does not refer to any specific drama. "Music for the Theatre," written for a small orchestra, is a suite of five pieces: Prologue, Dance, Interlude, Burlesque, and Epilogue. The jazz idiom, a vogue of the day, probably made its first entry into Boston Symphony Hall with this composition; it is mainly employed here in the Dance. Philip Hale (*Boston Herald*, November 21, 1925) found that the suite was "a more important work than the symphony" by Copland that had been played in February, and commented that Copland "has much to say and knows how he should say it." He even excused the brief entrance of jazz and called "Music for the Theatre" "one of the most interesting of the modern works." Hale also noted the enthusiasm of the audience. Even S. M., in his review for the *Christian Science Monitor,* who found plenty of faults in Copland's score, was forced to acknowledge that it showed great progress beyond the symphony and that Copland revealed great skill in writing for a small orchestra, a more difficult task than writing for a large one.

The most flattering recognition of the work lay in the fact that it gained the attention and respect of the brotherhood of progressive American composers, to such a degree that the American Committee of the International Society for Contemporary Music selected it for performance at the International Festival at Frankfurt in July 1927. The only other American work heard there was Henry Gilbert's "Dance in Place Congo."

That young Aaron Copland had aroused in Koussevitzky a more than common interest was certain, for after the performance of two Copland scores Koussevitzky encouraged the composer to write a piano concerto. This commission was carried out in 1926, and on January 28, 1927, the new concerto had its first hearing in Boston, with Copland as soloist. The mixture of melancholy, gentle music with outbursts of furious passion characteristic of Copland's earlier works also dominates this concerto.

Of Copland's Piano Concerto, the *Boston Globe* (January 29, 1927) said that "no music heard . . . in the past fifteen seasons has created so great a sensation." This was not meant as a compliment to the composer. On the contrary, the reviewer spoke of the "scandal created by the wholly incidental use of saxophones . . . bits of jazz rhythm"; and he reported "a general appearance of stupefaction" in the public. Yet he acknowledged that the concerto sounded "like the early work of a man who may become a great composer." The critic of the *Boston Post* wrote, "Copland's latest is poor stuff," "a banal piece." Philip Hale found that in the Piano Concerto Copland was "on the wrong track," that there was "little to attract, little to admire, much to repel," that the concerto showed "a shocking lack of taste, of proportion." After the esteem he expressed for the "Music for the Theatre," Hale was gravely disappointed by the new work, and felt that "one should be sorry for Mr. Copland."

Copland contributed a smaller work, performed by Koussevitzky on December 14, 1928, called "Two Pieces for String Orchestra." They had originally been written as string quartet music and in this form had been heard in New York. Transcribed for string orchestra, this Lento and Rondino were given for the first time in Boston. The Rondino is based on a theme of which the single notes spell the name Gabriel Fauré—a procedure made possible only by a combination of the English and the French solfeggio names of the tones. This comparatively simple and unpretentious work shows us Copland in his gentler, more amiable mood.

Copland's contribution to the Orchestra's Fiftieth Anniversary was a "Symphonic Ode" which Koussevitzky introduced on February 19, 1931.* As a worthy tribute to the memorable occasion, the young composer designed a dignified, even monumental, piece in five sections, its pomp and grandeur relieved by two rapid intermezzi of a lighter character. Having the Boston Orchestra at his disposal, Copland was not modest or reticent in his demands. No less than eight horns, five trumpets, three trombones, two tubas, piano, two harps, glockenspiel, and all imaginable percussion instruments were added to the large string band and wood-winds ensemble in groups of four each. The basic motive of the piece is taken from an older Copland piece, a Nocturne for violin and piano.

On October 14, 1938, Koussevitzky conducted Aaron Copland's latest score, "El Salon Mexico." The name indicates how well Copland—a close and shrewd observer of what impresses the listening public—has understood the value of a suggestive title. Though he has no trust in the elaborate "programs" for symphonic works in vogue during the twenties, he is equally averse to the now fashionable reticence in the neo-classical camp. How

* Two of Copland's fellow students in Paris have written on the Ode: Thomas Chanler in *Hound and Horn* (Fall 1930), and Virgil Thomson in *Musical Quarterly* (January 1932).

much better a title like "El Salon Mexico" sticks to the memory than a modest "Music for Orchestra" or "Concertino" and the like! The composition is a brilliant orchestral setting of popular Mexican melodies, reminiscences of a journey to Mexico, and of contact with the modern Mexican public in a "hot spot" of the gay capital, called "El Salon Mexico." Copland has given us a real salon piece of ultra-fashionable type, pleasing the mass of the musical public by its slightly exotic tunes borrowed from Mexican song collections, and enlivened with pungent Mexican paprika sound, exciting dynamics, and insinuating rhythmical sting. However, the professional musician is also pleased with the sly skill and the command of the modern resources here displayed. One should not overrate the artistic value of so captivating a "piece of the month"; yet one can understand why a jury selected this "Salon" to represent the United States at the London Festival of the International Society for Contemporary Music in 1938—it meant a sure success. Leonard Bernstein, the youngest musical celebrity in America, also was similarly motivated when he included Copland's "Salon" in the program with which he achieved sensational success at his debut as composer and conductor of the Boston Symphony Orchestra, on February 18, 1944.

Copland's "Quiet City" was performed by Koussevitzky for the first time on April 18, 1941, and was repeated that same year at the Berkshire Festival in August, and in Boston in December. It shows, too, Copland's inclination for suggestive and impressive titles. This piece, surpassing in musical value "El Salon Mexico," took its title from a now forgotten play to which Copland contributed some incidental music. To turn this otherwise lost music to the best possible account, Copland salvaged some of the themes and expanded them into a symphonic piece for trumpet solo and English horn solo with string orchestra. Thus came into existence a very beautiful modern piece, offering a welcome and rare opportunity to a first-class trumpet player and an English horn virtuoso to distinguish themselves as soloists. Though the title has little connection with the music—which makes one think neither of a city nor of quiet—it is a well-sounding label and helps one to remember the piece. One may truthfully assert that the music also sounds uncommonly well for a modern piece, much more so than many another Copland composition, such as his Piano Variations with their yelling discords. "Quiet City" is even sentimentally appealing; there is a really fine symphonic duet of the two solo instruments, supported by a masterly treatment of string orchestra that at places also has an impressive part in the dialogue. The small body of instruments employed yields surprisingly rich and refined sonorities, proof of the composer's superior art and highly developed individual taste. Georges Mager and Louis Speyer, the first trumpet and English horn players of the Boston Orchestra, played the solo parts with accomplished art at all three performances.

A naïve foreigner, on seeing Copland's ballet "Billy the Kid" would learn with surprise that Billy the Kid was one of America's most ruthless cowboy bandits and killers, and that the ballet glorifies the violent life of this Wild West hero. Perhaps he might ask whether this is a typically American story, and what music has to do with it. Evidently Copland asked himself the same questions, and evidently he did find something typically American in this tale and something fit for musical treatment. As a musician, Copland is concerned with Americanism in its various phases, but also with the dignity of the art of music. Yet in this particular case, one may suspect that commercial reasons prompted him to neglect the dignity of music, as he is otherwise not a specialist in stories appealing to the instincts of the prize ring. A "Suite from Billy the Kid, Character Ballet" was conducted by Richard Burgin at a Boston concert on January 30, 1942, and the audience duly appreciated its breezy and strong popular music: "The Open Prairie—Street in a Frontier Town—Card Game at Night—Gun Battle—Celebration after Billy's Capture." The Boston program book on the occasion contained extracts from an interview with Copland, published by the *New York Sun*. From it, one learns that Copland was intent on "getting rid of the idea that American music is a weak sister." He was certainly successful in this aim. "Billy the Kid" is American music in the robust teen age, a lusty, vigorous, youngster in which the Germans call its *Flegeljahre*. In his interview Copland also expressed the laudable opinion that American music had got "too far away from the public" and was being isolated. In the endeavor to write "simpler and more appealing music," Copland had his eyes "trained on radio, film, theater and ballet audiences, which seem to me more receptive and potentially more responsive than those of the concert halls." These revealing confessions give us the key to Copland's interesting and remarkable dual personality, a parallel to the Dukelsky-Vernon Duke case, mentioned elsewhere in this book. In his "Salon Mexico," his children's opera "The Second Hurricane," his film music, and "Billy the Kid," Copland exploited with gratifying financial and artistic success the popular, surface features of Americanism which appeal to the crowd. In his symphonic and chamber music, however, he is not averse to a sophisticated, highly pretentious *l'art pour l'art* point of view, and is ambitious to impress the exacting connoisseur with the intrinsic values of a distinguished musical art. Which of the two Coplands thus revealed will finally be accredited as the superior personality cannot at present be foreseen. Possibly—and this would be a very desirable aim—he may succeed in merging the two into one personality, combining artistic distinction and modernism with popular appeal.

The versatility of Copland is further seen in the fact that the same musician who exploited the crude Americanism of Billy the Kid had also aspired to interpret musically the loftiest representative of Americanism—Abraham Lincoln. On March 26, 1943, Koussevitzky conducted for the first time in Boston Copland's composition "A Lincoln Portrait." The Boston program notes give the following background: as World War II began, André Kostelanetz had the idea of discovering what music could do "to mirror the magnificent spirit of our country." The outcome of his idea were three "portraits" for orchestra, "Mark Twain" by Jerome Kern, "Mayor La Guardia" by Virgil Thomson, and "Lincoln" by Copland. The Lincoln portrait, certainly a noble piece, is one of Copland's most distinguished and remarkable works. He had the commendable idea of calling in the subject's assistance by having a speaker recite famous passages from Lincoln's speeches and writings. Around this declamation, finely done at the first performance by Will Geer the actor, the orchestra weaves thin threads of sound to provide an unobtrusive background and to underline certain important accents. Two orchestral preludes in symphonic style precede the final section. In the first one the composer aimed "to suggest something of the mysterious sense of fatality that surrounds Lincoln's personality" and "something of his gentleness and simplicity of spirit." The intermezzo in quick time is meant to sketch briefly "the background of the times he lived in." With the help of a good intuition and considerable technical skill these aims are well attained.

During the season 1945–1946, two recent compositions of Copland so far unknown in Boston were heard. Both of a popular type, they yet represent two different classes. The "Danzon Cubano," part of a program conducted by Leonard Bernstein on March 22, 23, 1946, is a companion piece to the above mentioned "Salon Mexico." It shows the composer as an attentive tourist in Cuba, greatly interested in the national dance form of the rhythmically, highly spiced Cuban "Danzon," and brilliantly paraphrasing his impressions. He is not intent on a genuine piece of exotic folklore, but rather on an effective modernistic number for the pretentious night club.

The Suite from the Ballet "Appalachian Spring" (played on October 5, 6, 1945) is of a much more elevated character. In fact, I am inclined to call it one of Copland's most valuable and truly beautiful works. For its first setting as a ballet for the outstanding dancer Martha Graham, the work was honored both by the Pulitzer Prize and by the award of the Music Critics' Circle of New York. Here we see Copland at his American best. Never has American folklore been better understood, more intensively felt, and more directly and simply translated into terms of a noble, yet popular art. A purified taste prevails throughout the score, in which attractive melodic material is finely balanced by an appropriate technical treatment in form, harmony, and orchestration. Not hunting for modernistic effect, the score yet finds that sort of convincing effect accessible only to a master of his art.

The first appearance of the name Roy Harris on a Boston Symphony program (January 26, 1934) is of special significance —comparable to the meaning of Copland's debut for American music ten years earlier. In Harris' music is seen a new American- ism; one of a more mature type than had so far been perceived; one less intent on the materialistic outlook, the skyscrapers, auto- mobiles, radio, jazz antics with twisted tunes, funny squeaking sounds, and crazy dance rhythms; an Americanism that relied instead on the spiritual and emotional fundaments of the Ameri- can soul. New York, Broadway, Tin Pan Alley, and Hollywood have contributed little or nothing to the art of Harris. He is, however, indebted to the English folksongs and dance tunes of the American West and South. To his thematic material Harris applies a constructive art of uncommon severity, based on classi- cal polyphony, an art of linear rather than coloristic values that is often reminiscent of diatonic Gregorian church modes but averse to the chromatic charms of romantic harmony. Fugue, canon, passacaglia structure mean much to him. Three years of study with Nadia Boulanger in Paris converted him neither to Debussy's and Ravel's impressionism nor to Stravinsky's neo- classicism.

Harris was more than thirty years of age before he gained serious attention in America with a number of chamber music works. Koussevitzky must be credited with recognizing the possi- bilities of Harris as a symphonic writer earlier than any other conductor. He was considerably impressed by Harris' first sym- phonic score of large dimensions, "Symphony: 1933" which he performed for the first time from the manuscript on January 26, 1934. In speaking of this work, Koussevitzky called it "the first truly tragic symphony by an American." Harris himself has described the contents of this symphony in the Boston program book as follows: "In the first movement I have tried to capture the mood of adventure and physical exuberance; in the second, of the pathos which seems to underly all human existence; in the third the will to power and action." It would indeed be hard to think of a prominent contemporary American composer other than Harris to whom one might feel justified in ascribing such

a program. Almost everybody else would have considered such
an attitude as old-fashioned, un-American emotionalism, not
in accord with the realistic, unsentimental modernism of our
age.

After an eminently successful introduction to Boston with his
first symphony, Harris could count on Koussevitzky and the
Orchestra as unsurpassed helpers in his career. In the following
season, on February 28, 1936, his Second Symphony had its first
performance in a concert that Richard Burgin conducted. Unlike most of his American colleagues, Roy Harris is vigorously
active as his own publicity agent, and he contributed to the
Boston program book a detailed, precise, and useful analysis of
his new symphony. The first movement, "Con bravura," is an
exuberant piece, entirely evolved from the initial motive of four
notes, somewhat as is the first movement of Beethoven's Fifth
Symphony. After an introduction on the four notes, in which
they are juggled about in various ways, the main theme is heard
four times, each time somewhat varied; once it is written in strict
canon, once in a freer, ornamental type of canon. The vigorous
bravura of the movement is wisely relieved by an episode of a
gentler nature, a moment of meditation, confided to the English
horn—the favorite instrument of recent American composers for
such darkly tinged, serious, and somewhat melancholy solilo-
quies. The entire first movement was intended as an elaborate
prelude to the next two movements.

The second movement, Molto cantabile, is based on a theme
which the composer calls polytonal, not because several tonalities are heard simultaneously but because the theme itself "shifts
its tonal center many times." The bulk of this piece consists of
various types of canons, a contrapuntal form with which Harris
is most seriously preoccupied in many works. The canon is favorable to a "contemplative mood," attained in this piece.

To this "study in canons" Harris opposed "a study in rhythmic developments" in the finale, superscribed Maestoso. Here
stretches of the music are dominated successively by the dotted
half note, the plain half note, the half plus quarter, the quarter,
and lastly the eighth note. This arithmetical scheme produces a

vivacity which constantly intensifies from the stately beginning until it achieves a rather rapid pace. After these evolutions "the movement tightens constantly," and in the coda there is, as a logical consequence, a combination of eighth, quarter, and half notes. The composer intended to evolve "a feeling of power" from these rhythmic exercises, and certainly considerable intellectual power is here displayed. Whether the expressive and emotional powers are equally convincing is a question that can be finally answered only after one has more thorough acquaintance with this original symphony than can be obtained from a single performance.*

Aaron Copland, Harris' colleague and rival, defends Harris (*American Mercury*, April 1935) against certain attacks, pointing out Harris' striking melodic gift and claiming that his music realizes a characteristically American melos more strikingly than do the works of any other American composer. He analyzes the sources of Harris' melody, the Celtic folk tunes and the Protestant hymn tunes.

Harris' Third Symphony, performed by Koussevitzky for the first time on February 24, 1939, was the sensation of the season 1938–1939 as far as American music was concerned. It was heard again on October 6, 1939, made a profound impression at the Berkshire Festival, August 3, 1940, and was repeated a fourth time on December 26, 1941. Universally this Third Symphony was considered the most important work yet produced in the symphonic field in America; and in the season 1941–1942 no less than thirty-three performances by American orchestras are recorded, besides performances in Mexico and London. The composer himself wrote for the Boston program book a brief, instructive table of contents and plan of its structure, which are indicative of his clarity of thought and his intellectual though not unemotional approach to music. The symphony, written in one continuous movement, has five distinct sections:

* Readers interested in Harris' music and his theories about it may refer to an essay by him, "American Music Enters a New Phase," in *Scribner's Magazine*, October 1934, and to another of his articles, published in the *Musical Quarterly*, April 1934.

I. Tragic—bow string sonorities.
II. Lyric—strings, horns, wood winds.
III. Pastoral—emphasizing wood-wind color.
IV. Fugue—dramatic, brass . . . percussion dominating . . .
V. Dramatic—Tragic.

The symphony reaches its culmination in the powerful and striking fugue finale.

In his Folk-Song Symphony for Chorus and Orchestra, Harris fully lived up to his belief in a national art based on folksong. He had the advantage of working in an age that had made the first discovery of America's immense wealth of folklore, as seen in the extensive literature on folksongs and in collections of many thousands of indigenous tunes in the Library of Congress. As explained by Harris in the Boston program book, when Koussevitzky directed the new score on February 21, 1941, his new tendency here was "to bring about a cultural cooperation and understanding between the High School, college and community choruses of our cities with their symphonic orchestras." Accordingly, he selected a number of tunes from the collections of J. A. Lomax and Carl Sandburg as his thematic material, which he treated with some freedom. The plan of the symphony provides five choral pieces and two instrumental interludes: "Welcome Party" is a choral setting of the tune "When Johnny Comes Marching Home," on which Harris had previously written his popular Overture. "Western Cowboy" deals with two tunes: "Oh Bury Me Not on the Lone Prairie," know as "The Dying Cowboy"; and "As I Walked Out in the Streets of Laredo." The gay, pathetic, and nostalgic melodies heard thus far are followed by the first interlude, "Dance tunes for strings and percussion," equivalent to a scherzo. Here a medley of Harris' own tunes, reminiscent of a hillbilly fiddler's tunes, is presented. "Mountaineer's Love Song," corresponding to the lyric slow movement of a symphony, treats a song of British origin, which is given mountaineer and southern Negro touches—"I'm goin' away for to stay a little while." Another lively interlude on popular tunes is written as a change for the full orchestra. A "Negro Fantasy," for chorus based on "Moanin'," an old hymn—"De trumpet sounds it in my soul"—is an arresting, very original piece treated in "camp-meeting fashion." The finale, "If ever I travel this road again," is a cowboy's longing for "the gal I left behind me." Harris added the phrase "Good night" as a coda. The entire symphony is a noteworthy and successful attempt at promoting popular music without sacrificing the demands of serious art. The Cecilia Society Chorus, trained by Arthur Fiedler, participated in the Boston performance.

A microfilm copy of Harris' Folk-Song Symphony was officially sent by airplane to Soviet Russia as a representative American work; in exchange, the United States received a microfilm version of the Seventh Symphony of Shostakovich, which became a great sensation in America during the 1943 season.

Harris wrote his Fifth Symphony in 1942, and Koussevitzky conducted its first performance in Boston on February 26, 1943. This date had been carefully selected by Koussevitzky: in the same week Soviet Russia celebrated the twenty-fifth anniversary of the founding of the Red Army; moreover Harris had dedicated the new symphony to the USSR. For the Boston program book, Koussevitzky composed an inspired message "To the Red Army and the Red Fleet of Soviet Russia," part of which reads:

Mighty, unconquerable is the Red Army. But not in armor alone is her might: Her spirit is invincible. Fighting for the right cause, the leaders and warriors of the Red Army know that the whole Motherland is back of them; and back of the Motherland stands the wide, the brotherly world.

Harris' dedication of the Fifth Symphony also appeared in the program book, and the composer stated:

As an American citizen I am proud to dedicate my Fifth Symphony to the heroic and freedom-loving people of our great Ally, the Union of Soviet Socialist Republics, as a tribute to their strength in war, their staunch idealism for World peace, their ability to cope with stark materialistic problems of world order without losing a passionate belief in the fundamental importance of the arts.

In the program book also Harris clearly described the spiritual contents of his Fifth Symphony. He aimed to express certain fundamental features of the American character:

. . . qualities . . . which our popular dance music, because of its very nature, cannot reveal. Our people are more than pleasure-loving. We also have qualities of heroic strength—determination—will to struggle —faith in our destiny. We are possessed of a fierce driving power— optimistic, young, rough and ready—and I am convinced that our mechanistic age has not destroyed an appreciation of more tender moods. And it is right that these gentler moods should live in us. Otherwise our strength and vitality might degenerate into a ruthless brutality.

This apotheosis of Americanism, to be expressed in music, is a far cry from the materialistic Americanism of the twenties. It makes one think, too, of the aspirations and prophetic utterances made by Henry Gilbert fifteen years previously (see Chapter 6).

Harris explains that a martial spirit crept into the music almost without any premeditation on his part. This martial spirit especially animates the first movement, a rather brief prelude, unfolding directly, that is, without ever digressing into development sections.

The second movement is a broad chorale, "in singing choral style, yet rhapsodic"; more precisely, several "chorals of hope and peace" unfold and intertwine in the course of the austere yet sublime piece. The plan provides for a gradual rise of the first melody to the very highest register of the violins, soaring above a chorale in the brass and wood winds. This chorale, too, is led upwards to its culmination by the violas and cellos. From this climax a gradual descent is brought about, leading to a new extended chorale section, in antiphonal dialogue between muted strings and resounding brass and wood wind.

The finale is a triple fugue, in three sections on three themes, intermixed with rondo features. An added complication appears in the second section, where the second theme is developed as a double fugue in itself, on two different subjects. This complex fugue finale is certainly not meant to express the "pleasure loving" Americans referred to in the composer's dedication, but it might well stand for the American "determination, will to struggle, fierce driving power, rough and ready" character, whereas the chorale of the second movement expresses the "faith in our destiny, mixed with some of the more tender moods."

Roy Harris' Sixth Symphony, Opus 60, had been commissioned by the Blue Network in 1943, but it had its first performance at Boston Symphony Hall, conducted by Koussevitzky, on April 14, 1944. The score is dedicated "With Respect, to the Armed Forces of Our Nation," and it is based on Lincoln's Gettysburg Address. There are curious coincidences tying Roy Harris to Lincoln. Harris' birthday is February twelfth, as is Lincoln's, and he was born in Lincoln County, Oklahoma. The Gettysburg Address has accompanied him through most of his life; from his years in school, when he had to learn and recite it, to the years of his maturity, when he pondered over its meaning and came to understand its greatness through his own experiences. Thus it was by no means surprising that he should turn to the Gettysburg Address as the worthiest theme, when he resolved to write a new symphony weighty and exalted enough to be a tribute to the nation's armed forces at a time when world-shaking events were involving the United States in fateful decisions.

In a thoughtful explanation of the Symphony's contents, in the Boston program book, the composer states that he found in the Gettysburg speech "a classic expression of that great cycle which always attends any progress in the intellectual or spiritual growth of a people," namely: Awakening, Conflict, Dedication, Affirmation. Accordingly he gives these titles to the four movements of his Symphony. As he analyzes these titles, he shows just how he extracted them from the Gettysburg speech. "Awakening" refers to the beginning of Lincoln's address, a retrospective glance at the Revolution and the beginning of America's independence. "Conflict," of course, refers to the Civil War. "Dedication" is based on Lincoln's homage to the dead, when he said, "We have come to dedicate a portion of that field as a final resting place for those who here gave their lives that that nation might live." The composer calls this movement "a long chorale of dedication to the dead." "Affirmation" points to the concluding paragraph of the address, where Lincoln affirmed that "these sacrifices shall not have been made in vain," that "this nation, under God, shall have a new birth of freedom, and that government of the people, by the people, for the people, shall not perish from the earth."

To this finale the composer gives the form of a fugue, in order to "reflect in architectural terms the mood of strong faith in mankind."

This review of the symphony deals only with its plan and the ideas animating it. To appraise the music itself properly, the author would have liked a much closer familiarity with the score than could be gained at a single performance. A printed score of this important work is not yet available, but this much can be said: Harris' Sixth Symphony is more than the work of a talented musician. Here speaks a man filled with great ideas, not aspiring to achieve success cheaply, by catering to the prevalent taste of the epoch, but striving to guide the too-often misguided taste of America's friends of music to purer heights. It may be Roy Harris' mission to champion the dignity of music in America. The Sixth Symphony is certainly program music, but what a program! And how different in its spiritual elevation from the materialistic, low point of view of many pretentious American pieces that paint sensational features of American life!

Another memorable event of the 1938–1939 season was the introduction to Boston of a little-known young composer, William Schuman, who in subsequent years rose to a leading position in American music that made him a potent rival of Harris and Copland. Schuman, born in New York City in 1910, received his musical education at Columbia University and as a private pupil of Charles Haubiel and Roy Harris. He was also enrolled at the Mozarteum Academy in Salzburg in 1935. Schuman first claimed a certain amount of public attention in 1937, when his Second Symphony was awarded the prize in a nationwide competition for a new symphonic work. Copland, Harris, Wagenaar, and Sessions were the judges responsible for Schuman's leap into prominence. In 1938 the new symphony was heard twice in New York. It soon aroused Koussevitzky's interest, and was performed in Boston on February 17, 1939, gaining considerable attention on account of its youthful energy, its constructive power. The composer contributed to the Boston program book a rather detailed technical analysis of this unpublished work, which should be helpful to the student.

Schuman has publicly withdrawn from circulation a number
of his earlier works, including the Second Symphony, and it remains to be seen what the symphony will look like in its final
shape. One may speculate, for instance, on the fate of the tone
C, around which a great part of the symphony is built, and may
wonder whether this pivot will be strengthened or weakened.
The work, written in one extended movement, is based not only
on the tone C but also on a principal theme, played by the bass
instruments after the initial call to attention—dialogue of the
trumpets on the basic C. All three sections of the symphony
derive from the principal theme. This thematic economy, along
with the insistence on contrapuntal development, the predilection for ostinato figures and structural devices like strict canon,
plus the austerity of the music, point to the influence of Roy
Harris. Yet upon hearing the Second Symphony, one could have
no doubt concerning the as yet half-developed powers of Schuman—a new personality, a new force in American music.

After a successful debut in Boston, Schuman attained the
coveted distinction of becoming a regular guest there. On October 4 and 6, 1939, Koussevitzky opened the season with two extra
programs devoted exclusively to American works: Suite in E
major, Opus 63, by Arthur Foote; "Through the Looking-Glass,"
by Deems Taylor; Angelus from Third Symphony, by Henry
Hadley; "Skyscrapers," by John Alden Carpenter; Romantic
Symphony, by Howard Hanson; Piano Concerto, by George
Gershwin; Third Symphony, by Roy Harris; and Second Symphony, by Randall Thompson. The sole novelty among these
repetitions of works that were already well known was William
Schuman's "American Festival Overture." It was heard for the
first time on this occasion, for which it had been expressly composed. Success was assured by its popular appeal. The piece is
animated by the boisterous and joyful spirit of modern American youth, a shade of Americanism not previously exploited.
Here we meet the teen-age boys of New York City in rough, yet
good-natured play, without the trimmings of jazz, skyscrapers,
burlesque and rustic folksongs. Although not great music in the
strict sense of the term, this overture teems with talent. One can

see that a piece like Schuman's Overture gathers up the threads dropped when Henry Gilbert departed from the American scene in 1928.

Schuman's Third Symphony, introduced by Koussevitzky on October 17, 1941, is dedicated to him. It was awarded the first prize by the Music Critics' Circle of New York City, as the outstanding composition of the season 1942–1943. The unconventional plan of construction, with its exclusive use of old contrapuntal forms, shows the influence of Roy Harris. The first part of the symphony couples a passacaglia with a fugue, the second part a chorale with a toccata.

The passacaglia theme is not satisfied with a plain statement, as is found, for example, in the finale of Brahms's Fourth Symphony. It calls for assistance on the contrapuntal device of strict four-part canon. This highly involved theme is followed by five variations, with intermezzi as transitions between them. The fugue theme, vigoroso, has thematic as well as structural relations to the passacaglia. The theme, first played by the horns, is taken up by various instruments in a well-organized manner. First the strings take it up, singly in descending order; then follow successively violas and cellos, basses and tuba, wood winds, trombones, and lastly the trumpets. The seven entries of the theme disregard the classical tonic-dominant order, each one replacing it with unorthodox order of rising semitones—from B flat, through B natural, C, C sharp, D, E flat, and E. This scheme corresponds to the structure of the passacaglia, where the theme's successive entries also are in semitones, but in the reverse order —downward from E to B flat. In the further development the device of canon is amply exploited. A novel feature is the introduction of three variations into a fugue. This movement is one of the most ingenious and contrapuntally involved pieces ever penned in America, and it commands respect for its linear and polyphonic art coupled with characteristic thematic invention.

Part 2 of the symphony starts with a chorale, entering in the solo trumpet, after a brief introduction played by violas and cellos. The chorale melody is evolved from the passacaglia theme. Further symphonic treatment of the chorale leads over to the toccata, a brilliant finale, in which the *moto perpetuo* idea of the toccata form is skillfully exploited. Here again canon is much in evidence. Conspicuous features are a kind of rapid cadenza for the entire string band, and an ingenious thematic coda.

Schuman's contribution to the Boston season 1942–1943 was a secular cantata for chorus and orchestra, "A Free Song," heard for the first time under Koussevitzky's direction on March 26. Parts of three poems by Walt Whitman, most American of all the nation's poets, were selected by the composer as fitting text for "A Free Song." The composer took the title from Whitman's "Song of the Banner at Daybreak," an inspired apostrophe to liberty written at the time of the Civil War, and just as applicable in 1943 when again a struggle was being waged for liberty. Schuman's choral setting is vigorous, grimly determined, swelled by pride, and at the close jubilant. It is liberally seasoned with tangy discordant modern harmony. The Harvard Glee Club and the Radcliffe Choral Society lent their fresh, young voices to the task with their usual enthusiasm. "A Free Song" was awarded the Pulitzer Prize in 1943.

Repeated reference has been made to the Koussevitzky Music Foundation established in memory of Mme. Natalie Koussevitzky. This Foundation has given a strong incentive to a number of gifted composers and has enriched the literature of recent American symphonic music with a number of weighty scores, such as Martinu's First Symphony, Berezowsky's Fourth Symphony, and Lopatnikoff's Concerto for orchestra. The latest addition to this list is William Schuman's Symphony for Strings, performed by Koussevitzky for the first time on November 12, 1943, and repeated on December 27. The first movement, Molto agitato ed energico, stresses vigor and excitement by its striking and plastic principal theme, played in unison by all violins on the G string, fortissimo. The manner of its treatment, in strong though rough harmony, in rhythmic bustle, intensifies the qualities inherent in the theme. The second movement, Larghissimo, starts with a striking series of broad chords, fortissimo but con sordino, presenting an interesting polytonality like a six-part double chorus, with its three upper voices in pure triads, its three lower voices also in pure triads but in a different key. The third movement, Presto leggiero, combines the scherzo with the finale character. It makes use of the rondo form, with variation of the humorous, slightly jazzy principal theme every time it reappears. This score does not give the impression of a string quartet transcribed for string orchestra, it lacks the polyphonic subtlety and complicated texture of a classical string quartet. An orchestra in tutti is intended to play this music, and in a style more homophonic than polyphonic, all instruments moving simultaneously in a chain of chords or in the same rhythmic patterns.

A shorter work by Schuman, "Prayer in Time of War," had its first Boston performance by Koussevitzky on October 6, 1944. This serious piece in one movement reveals strikingly the characteristic traits of the young composer. He disclaims any programmatic, descriptive tendencies, stating that the title is "merely an indication of the kind of feeling that went into the composition."

During the season 1940–1941 a young man of thirty was introduced to the Boston public, who five years later took his place in the front rank of American composers. Samuel Barber, educated at the Curtis Institute in Philadelphia, the winner of the Prix de Rome in 1935 and of two Pulitzer prizes, came to public attention in a larger measure for the first time in 1938, when Toscanini performed his Adagio for Strings—subsequently one of the most played modern pieces—and his "Essay for Orchestra."

The first work of Barber heard at Koussevitzky's Boston concerts was the Overture to *The School for Scandal,* on November 15, 1940. This score, as well as his other works, revealed a composer who mastered modern technical means yet abstained from all such modernistic traits as atonality, twelve-tone technique, motoric and burlesque music, jazz, polytonality, neo-classicism, impressionism, constructivism, and linear counterpoint. Barber reminds one of Richard Strauss in his brilliant orchestral writing, his liking for melody—even tunefulness—his occasional exhibition of romantic emotionalism. His music captivates the public more than that of any other leading American composer. Yet outspoken Americanism is rarely if ever apparent. Though there is hardly anything novel in what he writes, his pieces are decidedly modern in effect and satisfying in their finished form and skillful blending of various modern ingredients. One might call him eclectic, but his eclecticism is of the pleasant, not of the repulsive, kind. In its gaiety, lightness, and speed the Overture reveals its descent from certain Mendelssohn scherzos and overtures.

"Essay for Orchestra" was introduced to Boston by Koussevitzky on April 25, 1941. One might call this "Essay" a sinfonietta in one movement for a large orchestra. It is a diverting and interesting piece, readily apprehended by anyone fairly well versed in modern harmonic devices.

Barber's skillfully and smoothly written Violin Concerto, first heard in Philadelphia with Albert Spalding as soloist, was twice performed by Koussevitzky—at the Berkshire Festival in August 1941 and on March 6, 1942, in Boston. At these performances the versatile and brilliant Ruth Posselt played the solo part. One listens with interest to so effective and impressive a piece, but the memory retains little; perhaps this is so because the music does not provoke much resistance from the listener. It carries him along pleasantly, yet poses no problems, awakens no contradiction during its smooth and polished progress. Though satisfying to normal taste, this music does not stimulate sufficiently; with its many positive qualities, this may be its weak point.

Barber's Second Symphony, Opus 19, "Dedicated to the Army Air Forces," is an outcome of the composer's experiences as a member of the air forces in Fort Worth, Texas. It had its first performance in Boston, on March 3, 1943, when Koussevitzky conducted it. Though the composer asserts that his symphony is not program music, the listener is in many places reminded of the "air," not only in the ordinary sense as the acoustic medium of sound but also in the sense of the vast space of open air, the medium of the airplane. This atmospheric outlook is suggested to the imagination especially in the second movement, an andante in a calm notturno mood. An English horn solo sings its melancholy tune in 4/4 time, on a background of ostinato rhythms in 5/4 time—a strange effect of unbalanced motion, not firm as on the ground, but suspended, as if in mid-air. This impression is strengthened at the culmination of this section when a novel instrument, so far unheard of in the orchestra, suddenly emits its strange sounds, an electrical "tone generator" especially built for this composition by the Bell Telephone Laboratories. It is meant to simulate the effect of a radio beam, an acoustic signal used in night flying. This signal motive is thematically exploited, taken up by other instruments, finally fading in the echo of two muted trumpets.

The finale also utilizes airplane experiences, in the manner in which the spiral figures in the presto introduction shoot upwards, while *terra firma* represented by the brass group asserts itself in occasional reply. The main part of the finale is a theme with variations and a fugato on an ostinato bass, in passacaglia manner. At the close the spiral figures reappear, perhaps this time suggesting, by the enlargement of the figure in the brass, the landing of the aircraft.

A small occasional piece by Barber was heard on October 29, 1943. This was a Commando March, originally written for military band, but at Koussevitzky's suggestion arranged by the composer as a brilliant and effective piece for orchestra.

Barber's latest work heard in Boston was his Concerto for Violoncello and Orchestra, Opus 22, played by that eminent mistress of her instrument, Raya Garbousova, on April 5, 6, 1945. Evidently the work was written expressly for her with a view to her exceptional powers. The irresistible enthusiasm with which she swept over its most exacting pages made it clear that she had made this score her own and defended it with utmost vigor. The composition is full of attractive and interesting episodes, but nevertheless open to attack. Its mixture of fantastic, romantic, lyric ideas lacks that unity of style, that logical coherence of structure which alone give a work the power of permanence and the rank of a classic—which after all is, or ought to be, the goal of every composer aspiring to the heights of art. This concerto was honored by the award of the New York critics for 1945.

For the first time the work of a Negro composer was played by the Boston Symphony Orchestra when George Szell, guest conductor, performed William Grant Still's "In Memoriam" on January 19, 1945. This composition was instigated by an invitation sent to seventeen composers in 1943 to write short orchestral works with reference to the second World War. The score of Grant Still is a noble tribute to "The Colored Soldiers Who Died for Democracy." In its style it mixes heroic and elegiac accents with traits suggestive of a funeral march. Still is not only one of the most gifted and accomplished composers of his race but also a respected member of the larger American brotherhood of creative musicians.

The musical celebrities of radio have not fared very well with Koussevitzky. They have had to wait for the rare intervals when Richard Burgin or some visiting conductor has placed some of their works on the Boston programs. Thus it was at a performance conducted by the famous Greek musician Dimitri Mitropoulos on December 15, 1944, that one found for the first time on a Boston program the name of Morton Gould, with his "Spirituals" for string choir and orchestra. These five pieces, "Proclamation—Sermon—A Little Bit of Sin—Protest—Jubilee," display an Americanism of the most outspoken manner, having a skillful, interesting, and impressive mixture of traits characteristic of white and Negro spirituals with jazz, boogie-woogie, and so on. "Our spirituals," the composer writes, "develop a wide gamut of emotions musically. Those emotions are specifically American. The songs range from ones that are escapist in feeling, or light and gay, to those having tremendous depth and tragic impact." The strings in this score represent the parts of a vocal choir. The tunes are confided mainly to them, while the wood-wind and brass orchestra and a plentiful assembly of percussion provide the characteristic background and proper atmosphere. It is worth mentioning that the "Spirituals" of this widely known radio conductor and composer were among the representative American works sent on microfilm to Russia in exchange for Russian scores.

Oscar Levant's name is well known to many American music lovers from his radio activities and records and from his many performances of Gershwin's "Rhapsody in Blue." A brilliant pianist and representative of Broadway and Hollywood music, Levant also has had interest in serious music. For some time he studied with Schönberg and took pains to penetrate the secrets of his intricate music. Richard Burgin, at a Boston concert on March 2, 1942, introduced two works by Levant to the Symphony Hall public. One of them, Overture 1912, is so named for no particular reason; it is not even faintly related to Tchaikovsky's boisterous 1812 Overture. If asked why he had chosen the whimsical title 1912, Levant would probably answer, "Why not 1912?" Levant has called this overture a kind of escape from the modernistic high-brow music with which he had been occupied for a time. Though professedly written for his own amusement, it has given amusement to many people, as proved by numerous performances under various conductors.

The second Levant piece in Burgin's program was the Dirge in which he lamented the premature death of his close friend and companion George Gershwin. Sincere and touching, this Dirge pays a worthy tribute to the extraordinary musician whose memory it extols.

The name of Paul Creston first appeared on a Boston program on January 24, 1944, when Vladimir Golschman as guest conductor presented Creston's Pastorale and Tarantella. The composer had recently gained considerable publicity when the Music Critics' Circle of New York City had chosen his First Symphony as the outstanding novelty of the 1943 season. Born in New York City in 1906, Paul Creston received his musical education there and so far he has confined his musical activities to New York. At present he is active as a church organist and as musical director for the Blue Network. The latter affiliation has naturally influenced his productions, as may be seen in such unusual combinations as a Concertino for Marimba and Orchestra and a Concerto for Saxophone and Orchestra. But lately he has passed beyond the field of radio music and has entered the concert hall in competition for symphonic honors.

His Pastorale and Tarantella is a variant of the widely used combination of introduction or prelude with a main piece. The Pastorale has a single theme. The Tarantella, a brilliant, effective piece, has larger proportions and is more dramatic in character. The violent, even wild motion of the tarantella dance is utilized with considerable skill. This piece shows the up-to-date combination of almost popular themes with modernistic trimming.

Another Creston work was heard in Boston when André Kostelanetz as guest conductor included Creston's "Frontiers" in his program on March 24, 1944. The saga of American migration to the West is here used not as the subject matter of a piece of descriptive program music but as an incentive, a guide to a composition that can well be understood and appreciated as absolute music. The main ideas—the vision, the trek, the achievement—must have suggested to the composer the character of his musical themes as well as the manner of their treatment. The principal theme, first stated by a muted trumpet, is suggestive of a still vague and dim vision; it dominates the entire composition in ever changing forms and variants, and thus it becomes the expression of endurance and tenacity. The second, principal section, corresponding to the "trek," is meant to convey "the sense of drive, of building, surmounting of increasing difficulties." The final section deals with the "achievement," giving musical expression of satisfaction, gratefulness at the completion of a huge job, and mixing with it "a renewal of the original vision for even greater accomplishment." The piece, in its entire conception, indicates a not too common insight into the relation of ideas and events to music, and it can be rated as a legitimate and promising application, in a modern sense, of program music.

In his Second Symphony, Opus 35, Paul Creston intended to present "an apotheosis of the two foundations of all music: song and dance." It begins with an introduction containing four successive themes, of which the first two are the thematic source of whatever occurs in the symphony. Variations by the dozens, inversions, rhythmical transformations of the main themes, in a very complex structure strive to give organic coherence to the composition. The attempt is laudable, but Creston did not succeed in making the greatly complicated score appear natural, simple, and enjoyable to the ear. Ingenuity is not enough for a symphonic work aspiring to be called masterly, unless with it are linked a supreme ease and a melodic inspiration soaring above the effort of forcibly bending, twisting, and coupling motives without much regard for the ensuing sound effect. The first movement is entitled "Introduction and Song," the second movement "Interlude and Dance." Song and dance since the times of Haydn, Mozart, and Beethoven have always been the basis of all symphonic music, and there is hardly any need for emphasizing this combination as the *spiritus rector* of a new work. Less thematic complication and greater melodic freedom would have contributed greatly to the total impression of this labored symphony. The composer cannot complain of being neglected. His symphony, finished in the summer of 1944, had its first performance by Rodzinski with the New York Philharmonic-Symphony Orchestra in February 1945, its second at Boston, a few weeks later, on March 23, when Koussevitzky took great pains with the problematic yet interesting score.

For the first time a major work of David Diamond was heard in Boston when Koussevitzky, on October 13, 1944, conducted Diamond's Second Symphony. This composer, at present just thirty-two, has written an amazing number and variety of larger works, such as orchestral scores, chamber music, concertos, songs, and ballet music. Most of them have been performed, some of them published. Yet while his scores had aroused attention and discussion in New York, Rochester, Chicago, and San Francisco, David Diamond was a newcomer to the Boston public. His Second Symphony commands respect for its musicianly qualities, its seriousness of aim, for many arresting pages. Indeed, details and sections of the music provoke a high degree of expectancy, which is not fully satisfied by the total impression. Diamond here appears to be a composer of decided creative ability, technically well equipped, expert in the modernistic procedures, but one who has mastered his material more than himself. The balance between the pretentious, complex writing and the unmistakable, clarified expression of a new personality in American music has not yet been found. This need not imply that such a balance may not be found, if the ambitious young composer strives more for quality of individual expression, for slowly perfecting his works in formal construction, thematic invention and economy of means, than for quickly accumulating a multitude of half-perfected works. There is not much Americanism manifest in this absolute symphonic music, which in its emotional intensity is more closely related to the symphonic writing of composers like Hanson and Berezowsky than to the emotionally cool constructivism of the Stravinsky school. Diamond's recently performed "Rounds" for String Orchestra (April 5, 6, 1946) shows the young composer's capacities to better advantage and must be rated one of the most musicianly and accomplished scores in the mass of new American works.

The great sensation of the last few years in American music has been the meteoric rise of Leonard Bernstein. Within one season, 1943–1944, this little-known Boston musician acquired celebrity at the age of twenty-five. A graduate of Harvard College and the Curtis Institute, he attended during several summers Koussevitzky's classes in conducting at the Berkshire Music Center. There his manifold talents aroused Koussevitzky's special interest, an interest that helped Bernstein to obtain the position of assistant conductor to Rodzinski, of the New York Philharmonic-Symphony Orchestra. By fortunate circumstance he revealed his brilliant talents as a conductor in New York, and a short time later Koussevitzky invited him—a unique distinction—not only to conduct half a concert of the Boston Symphony Orchestra but at the same time to perform his symphony "Jeremiah."

This concert, on February 19, 1944, was a phenomenal success for both the conductor and the composer. "Jeremiah" has special significance in two ways: it is a remarkable piece of modern symphonic writing, though not yet a masterpiece; and it is a weighty contribution to the still young literature of Judaic music. His music reveals young Bernstein as a pupil of both Stravinsky and Ernest Bloch, and as a rival of Aaron Copland. This would indicate to a connoisseur of modern music the general nature of Bernstein's "Jeremiah" score even before he had heard it. Yet this score does not merely reëcho the voices of older masters, it also captivates the receptive listener's attention by its very

personal, persuasive, and sincere accent, and it justifies considera-
tion of its composer as one of the few welcomed in the ranks of
America's great art of music. After so promising a start, Leonard
Bernstein is under obligation to his own artistic standard, and it
will be a serious problem for him to live up to what severe
critics have a right to expect of him. The Music Critics' Circle
of New York City selected the "Jeremiah" score as the most remarkable novelty of the season 1944.

The three movements of "Jeremiah" are entitled "Prophecy—
Profanation—Lamentation." "Prophecy" is a serious, darkly
tinged piece intended—as the composer explains in the program
book—"to parallel in feeling the intensity of the prophet's pleas
with his people." It is intensely Jewish in accent, rhythm, and
melodic phrase, without, as the composer assures us, actually
employing Hebrew thematic material. The second movement,
"Profanation," however, makes use of a traditional Hebrew
chant. This almost savage, orgiastic scherzo is perhaps the most
striking part of the symphony. It paints in tones reminiscent of
Stravinsky's "Sacre" the revelry and corruption of the people of
Jerusalem that aroused the passionate wrath of the prophet
Jeremiah. In the last movement, "Lamentation," the most touching part of the symphony, the voice of the prophet himself appears in a sublime lament and exhortation from the original
Hebrew text. This vocal recitation utilizes a solemn liturgical
formula still used in the Jewish service on the days commemorat-
ing the destruction of the temple in Jerusalem and the Baby-
lonian captivity. Jenny Tourel of the Metropolitan Opera Company sang this Hebrew lamentation and found the right accent
and expression for her unusual task; her singing was a potent
factor in the undeniably profound impression of the symphony.

In the following season Leonard Bernstein was again invited
by Koussevitzky to conduct a concert in Boston, and at a Pops
Concert he also scored a considerable success as a pianist, playing
the Ravel concerto. In the meantime he had written the music for
the Broadway musical comedy *On the Town*, which proved to
be a hit of the New York season.

With all his activity as a conductor, pianist, and composer of serious and popular music, Leonard Bernstein has set up a record enviable at first glance. Yet there is this to consider: the history of music records a number of phenomenally gifted young composers who, after a triumphant, brilliant start, have lapsed into mediocrity and finally obscurity. Just as one cannot be prime minister to four different states at the same time, it seems that one cannot be simultaneously a master in many fields of art. Continued excellence in any branch of art demands even the most highly gifted individual's concentration of effort. To disperse one's talents too ambitiously can only lead in the long run to mediocrity in all fields or even collapse. The American public is too easily inclined to applaud achievements like those of Leonard Bernstein as a unique record of musical sportsmanship, as a victory in an all-round competition. But the records valid in sport and in art are by no means identical.

Lukas Foss is the youngest composer ever to have been considered worthy of having a work performed by the Boston Symphony Orchestra. Born in Berlin in 1922, educated at the Paris Conservatory from 1933 to 1937, he continued his studies at the Curtis Institute and at the Berkshire Music Center as a pupil of Hindemith and of Koussevitzky in conducting. He aroused Koussevitzky's interest to such a degree that his orchestral piece "The Prairie" was performed in Boston on October 15, 1943, and in the next year he was appointed successor to Sanromá as official pianist of the Boston Symphony Orchestra. As a pianist and as a composer he quickly succeeded in showing his extraordinary talents and capacities, so that at present he holds a place in the front rank of America's youngest musicians. His cantata for chorus and orchestra, "The Prairie," recently performed by Rodzinski with the New York Philharmonic-Symphony Orchestra, gained unanimous praise from the New York critics. As performed by Koussevitzky, "The Prairie" is not an extract from the cantata but a new piece based on themes of the cantata. It shows to best advantage the surprising maturity of the young composer in matters of form, orchestration, thematic invention, and ingenious development of his ideas. One has good reason to expect outstanding achievements from Lukas Foss.

CHAPTER 12

RETROSPECTIVE GLANCE

Looking over the list of the American works performed by Koussevitzky between 1924 and 1944, one finds that no less than sixty-six new American compositions were heard for the first time in Boston, and altogether one hundred and sixty-two American works were performed up to April 1944. To this number must be added the American works offered in the seasons 1944–1945 and 1945–1946, plus numerous works of "young" Americans who have only recently become citizens of the United States or who are about to achieve citizenship, men like Schönberg, Toch, Křenek, Milhaud, Castelnuovo-Tedesco, Bartók, Rachmaninoff, Stravinsky, Hindemith, Lourié, and others. In summary, the number of 150 American works is not exaggerated.

Study of the list also shows that Koussevitzky in his early years with the Orchestra had to rely mainly on older American composers like Foote, Chadwick, MacDowell, Loeffler, Hill, Gilbert, Hadley, Bloch, Converse, Carpenter, Mason, Goldmark, Taylor, and Schelling, because the younger, postwar generation had at that time too little suitable for a Boston Symphony program. Aaron Copland was the only representative of this younger generation in the years 1924–1926. He is at the top of the list, with eleven different works, some of which were several times repeated. In 1927 Copland was joined by Dukelsky, the second young composer of the list, with seven works over the years, and Alexander Lang Steinert, with three works. In 1927 Roger Sessions made his only appearance on the list. Walter Piston's name occurred for the first time in 1928; with a total of nine works he nearly equals the record of Copland, who may, however, boast of more repetitions.

In 1929 Howard Hanson first drew attention, and in the course of time his four symphonies were brought out in Boston. Nicolai Berezowsky made his Boston debut in 1931; a total of eight works makes him a close competitor with Copland and Piston. George Gershwin gained access to Boston Symphony Hall for the first time in 1932; his works add up to only three—quite naturally, as the theater was his domain rather than the concert hall. Leo Sowerby, a guest from Chicago, paid his first visit to Boston in 1932, returning twice in later years. Louis Gruenberg, also from Chicago, was heard for the first time in 1933 and again in 1939. In 1934 Roy Harris' first symphony was heard, followed by five other symphonies. Randall Thompson obtained a place on a Koussevitzky program for the first time in 1934; in 1940 his "Alleluiah" for chorus was added at the Berkshire Festival, and in 1945 his "Testament of Freedom." William Schuman made his extremely successful debut in 1939; his record totals five works in five years. Samuel Barber, next to William Schuman the youngest of the Boston favorites, appears for the first time in 1941; altogether five of his works were heard. Nicolas Lopatnikoff's five works were heard in 1928, and between 1939 and 1945. The youngest members of the young generation, David Diamond, Paul Creston, Leonard Bernstein, and Lukas Foss, came to the Boston front for the first time in 1944.

Of older American composers, still living and active, Edward B. Hill tops the list with twelve different works; next follows Ernest Bloch with nine; Carpenter with six; Eichheim and Werner Josten with three; Frederick Jacobi and David Diamond with two. About a dozen others had one performance only. The balance of the account shows Hill, Copland, Piston, Berezowsky, Harris, Hanson, Lopatnikoff, Schuman, and Barber as the main contestants for honors in the Boston area.

The season 1930–1931 is of special significance in any history of the Boston Symphony Orchestra because it marked the fiftieth anniversary of the Orchestra's founding in 1881. On this occasion Koussevitzky rendered a valuable service to contemporary music. He had the fortunate idea of commissioning a number of outstanding composers in various countries, as well as several American musicians, to write new works expressly for this festival season. Thus came into existence several works of great excellence, which otherwise probably would not have been written at all; at the same time new American symphonic music received a strong impetus through the encouragement given to highly gifted younger composers and through the wide publicity accorded their efforts. Ten works by American composers were heard during this season: two had been commissioned; one was heard for the first time in the United States; four were heard for the first time anywhere; the rest were works that had already been heard in Boston or elsewhere.

The fiftieth season was ushered in by a retrospective program. The very first concert of the Orchestra in 1881 was reproduced, having the same program, except for the final number, and the same conductor. George Henschel, who became the first conductor of the Orchestra in 1881, now Sir George Henschel, a high musical dignitary of Britain, at the age of eighty years had been invited to return from London to the American city of his early triumphs and to conduct the first concert of the jubilee season. Works by Beethoven, Gluck, Haydn, Schubert, Bach, and Wagner made up the program; Margaret Matzenauer was the soloist.

The second concert, on October 17, contained that now famous orchestral version of Moussorgsky's "Pictures at an Exposition," written by Ravel for Koussevitzky at the latter's suggestion. This brilliant and unmatched masterpiece of orchestration has frequently been performed by the Boston Symphony. The "Ode" by E. B. Hill, one of the new American works written for the occasion, was also part of this program.

In the third program, October 24, Roussel's G minor Symphony, Opus 42, commissioned by Koussevitzky, had its first hearing anywhere.

The fourth concert, on October 31, was ushered in by an Overture of an anonymous composer, heard for the first time and "written for the 50th Anniversary." It was an open secret that Koussevitzky himself was the composer of this overture. Included in the program was the first performance in America of a "Symphonie Lyrique" by the young Russian composer Nicolas Nabokov.

Another work written for the jubilee season was heard for

the first time anywhere at the fifth concert, on November 7. This was "Metamorphoseon, Modi XII," a theme with twelve variations, by the distinguished Roman composer Ottorino Respighi.

In the sixth concert, November 14, the first performance of Prokofieff's Fourth Symphony, Opus 47, "Composed for the Fiftieth Anniversary of the Boston Symphony Orchestra," was heard.

The seventh program, November 28, contained another American work commissioned by Koussevitzky, Howard Hanson's Romantic Symphony.

The next concert, conducted by Richard Burgin on December 12, acquainted Boston for the first time with a new work of the then phenomenally successful young Austrian composer Ernst Křenek—Little Symphony, Opus 58.

On December 19 Koussevitzky conducted one of the most remarkable concerts of the entire season. The two great leaders of modern music, Stravinsky and Schönberg, who personally are violently opposed to each other, were here peacefully coupled in the same program. One of Stravinsky's major works, the "Symphonie de Psaumes," written for the anniversary season, was heard for the first time in America. It was followed by Stravinsky's new Capriccio for Piano and Orchestra, likewise unknown in America until then. Jesús María Sanromá, the Orchestra's brilliant pianist, a specialist in modern music, was particularly excellent in this task. Schönberg's rich orchestral setting of Bach's Prelude and Fugue in E flat for organ concluded this memorable concert.

On January 2, 1931, the first American performance of Arthur Lourié's "Sonate liturgique," in the form of four chorales, took place. A small chorus of alto voices trained by Arthur Fiedler participated. Lourié is the author of the first biography of Koussevitzky, published in New York in 1931.

Sanromá distinguished himself again on February 13, when he played the solo part of a Suite for Pianoforte and Orchestra by the young Neopolitan composer Mario Pilati. The same program offered the first performance anywhere of Honegger's new symphony, written at Koussevitzky's request for the anniversary season. Two older works of Loeffler completed this program.

Hill's Second Symphony was the novelty of the seventeenth concert, on February 27, 1931; another new American work, Steinert's "Leggenda Sinfonica," was heard a week later.

Hindemith's "Konzertmusik" for String and Brass Instruments, written at Koussevitzky's request for the Orchestra, was a feature of the twenty-first program, on April third.

The last novelty of this memorable season was "The Rio Grande," for chorus, orchestra, and solo pianoforte, a work of the young English composer Constant Lambert. Sanromá participated again, and the Cecelia Society chorus, trained and conducted by Arthur Fiedler, whose entire career is closely connected with the Boston Symphony, as viola player, celesta player, and permanent conductor of the popular summer concerts.

The works performed at Boston do not represent the average of the American production but the cream of the crop, fastidiously selected by Koussevitzky. This taste is also evident in what he rejected. The loud, aggressive sensationalism of composers like Edgar Varèse, George Antheil, Henry Cowell, Leo Ornstein did not appeal to him. Similarly, the extreme stubborn individualism of those strange old Yankee musicians Carl Ruggles and Charles E. Ives did not attract him, and he had little interest in the universally known celebrities of radio music—they did not need his patronage. Koussevitzky's cool judgment of artistic values and his independent appraisal of the American scene were not influenced by over-zealous publicity, by fashionable trends, by press campaigns, or by local or regional patriotism. He performed what he considered to be the best of all works produced in America. A critical examination of what has been produced, performed, and praised in America during the last two decades shows indeed how close Koussevitzky came to discovering the true values.

The present situation in America is in many ways a replica of that in Germany ten years earlier. From about 1920 to 1932 there was a prodigious outpouring of new "revolutionary" music all over Germany, new operas by the hundreds, immense numbers of chamber and orchestral scores. All this was passionately discussed in the press, torn to pieces by the conservative critics, excessively praised by progressive writers. To be a "young revolutionary" in itself meant a distinction, independent of artistic values. A cult of "youth," never equalled before, was the sign of the epoch. Yet fifteen years later only a small fraction of all this production survives—about a dozen works of Hindemith's ceaseless output, about as much of Ernst Toch's music, and of Křenek's sensational and prodigious activities even less is now known.

In America young musicians are at present feverishly active. The abundance of excellent symphony orchestras has greatly influenced them in certain directions. Virtuosity of orchestration has become a common achievement nowadays and free modern harmony and contrapuntal skill are everywhere displayed. Yet this technical proficiency is not equivalent or proportionate to higher artistic values. Symphonies are now written by the hundreds every year. Almost every conservatory student of composition graduates with a symphony; many of them are performed at least once; far too many win prizes and scholarships and high praise. Each year the New York critics crown a work as the best of the season, yet the best of the season may be very mediocre by the high standards of great art, and the publicity received in such cases will only serve to inflate mediocrity, to give the winners an exaggerated opinion of their importance. Americanism and youth are now trump cards, and an early success is easy enough. Yet how few scores survive even five years! The works greatly admired in the twenties ten years later had entirely disappeared from the programs. Consequently the question arises: What will be left by 1950 of our present prize-winning works? Is there one American master great enough to survive his early celebrity? Is there likely to appear anyone comparable to a Brahms, or even to a Dvořák, or a Grieg? Even though these queries cannot be answered, one can grant the probability that one or several outstanding masters will arise in the multitude of competitors. The quality of the works performed by Koussevitzky in Boston has given a decidedly hopeful outlook. Though many of them may be classed as mediocre, yet in the historical development even these lesser works deserve interest; they represent the stations on the road to artistic eminence. Great works, history teaches, do not grow in isolation. They are rather like the peaks in a chain of mountains, gradually rising above the hills. Without lesser good works *en masse* no great works are possible.

This insight into the genealogy of great art should somewhat reconcile one to the bustle, noise, and excitement in the camp of the new American music. If there emerges even one real master from all this turmoil, the labor expended will not have been in vain. And the present situation justifies the hope that there may be more than one or two creative personalities eminent enough to assume leadership in a brilliant new American school of music. The success of such a national school, however, depends on more than a number of highly gifted individuals and on patrons and helpers like Koussevitzky. To stabilize and perpetuate any attainments thus won, the support of the federal, state or municipal governments is also indispensable. The history of art has amply shown the great part everywhere played by government in a flourishing national art. Public opinion in America has so far considered art a private affair, a kind of business in which the state should not interfere. Yet the entire progress of the arts in this country points more and more clearly to the fact that for a national art the government, as the nation's representative, is in large measure responsible. To bring about such well-planned and efficient patronage, should be one of the next aims in the fight for a national school of American music.

CHAPTER 13

THE ARTIST KOUSSEVITZKY

To round off the picture of Koussevitzky as a great figure in contemporary music it remains to explain the nature of his art as a conductor and interpreter of the great works of music. Here a brief historical survey will be useful as a basis for our analysis.

The specialized art of what is now called orchestral conducting is a growth of the romantic nineteenth century. Even in the time of Beethoven a conductor in the modern sense hardly existed. As conductors, Bach, Haydn, and Mozart were chiefly concerned with performance of their own works. Moreover, the professional conductor—*kapellmeister, maestro di cappella,* as his ordinary title was—had his main field of action in the opera house. Concert orchestras on a larger scale came into existence only in the nineteenth century, and with them the obligation to perform a great variety of works by many different composers. This task demanded a new type of artist. He performed his own works rarely, as his regular task was to offer the public acknowledged masterpieces of musical literature and occasionally new works.

To the historically minded nineteenth century, the "literature" had become extremely important, and as elite scores became universally known and were repeatedly demanded by the public, "interpretation" of them became a new problem. The conductor had to be a scholar of the literature, had to busy himself with the details of "style," had to evolve an impressive "conception" of the masterpieces. As the music-loving public began to watch for the conception of a certain work by a conductor, it found a new intellectual sport in comparing it with the interpretations of other leading conductors. Thus certain standards were gradually built up, and a "tradition" was established. Next followed the competition of the conductors, who sought to surpass each other in brilliance, in effectiveness, and in showing off individuality of interpretation. Among them were traditionalists, and also modernists counteracting tradition and seeking a new approach to the presentation of a work of art. Schools were formed and specialists arose in the work of certain composers or in certain types of music. This development was natural, as all major orchestras had the same repertory, with slight deviations. The brief sketch given here suggests the entire history of conducting from about 1840 to 1940, from the time of Mendelssohn's activities with the Leipzig Gewandhaus Orchestra, Habeneck's leadership of the Paris Conservatory Orchestra, and Wagner's conducting at Dresden, to the time of the activities of Toscanini, Weingartner, Furtwängler, Bruno Walter, and Koussevitzky.

Proper appraisal and understanding of these great modern contemporary masters is contingent on familiarity with the achievements of their immediate predecessors, whose pupils they have been. Modern conducting began in Germany and Austria, stemming from Wagner, whose essay 'Über das Dirigieren' laid the foundation of the new art. It was his greatest disciple, Hans von Bülow, who first applied Wagner's teachings to the extended symphonic repertory. One should know, too, that the amazing technical virtuosity of almost all the world-famous conductors was acquired in the school of the theater. Arthur Nikisch, Anton Seidl, Felix von Weingartner, Arturo Toscanini, Karl Muck, Richard Strauss, Gustav Mahler, Bruno Walter, Wilhelm Furtwängler, Otto Klemperer, Georg Szell, and numerous others were opera conductors for many years before they acquired fame in the concert hall. Only in the twentieth century, especially in the Anglo-Saxon countries and in America, foreign to the world of opera, have a number of distinguished conductors had their training in the concert hall rather than the theater. Of these, Koussevitzky is the most eminent representative. Training that was unconventional particularly helped Koussevitzky to develop peculiar traits and an individual mentality that set him apart from his distinguished colleagues.

The earlier phases of Koussevitzky's professional education have been described in the first chapter of this book. There it has

been told that in the first decade of the present century the
unexcelled art of Arthur Nikisch in Berlin awoke in the mind
of the young double-bass virtuoso the ardent desire to achieve
something similar himself. After his apprentice years in Berlin
he was fortunate in getting the means to found his own orchestra
in Moscow. These Moscow years were the decisive period in
Koussevitzky's artistic growth. Not only did he acquire technical
mastery in the art of conducting, but also the ideas dominating
the philosophy of his art matured slowly in those years, about
1910 to 1918. He formulated his program, which was retained
all through his career. His truly catholic program embraced with
equal devotion the past, the present, and the future of the great
art of music. He aspired to a conservative ideal in the most accomplished rendering of the great, universally recognized masterpieces of the symphonic literature. To this was added a progressive tendency, through his active interest in the national as well
as international production. All new works of note performed
in Vienna, Paris, Berlin, London, he imported to Moscow, and
in his frequent concerts in those capitals he brought with
him the older and newer Russian music, Glinka, Tchaikovsky,
Moussorgsky, Borodin, Rimsky-Korsakoff, and the new works
of the younger generation: Scriabin, Glazounoff, Taneieff,
Liadoff, Stravinsky, and later the scores of the youngest class,
headed by Prokofieff. This national propaganda was greatly
strengthened by a publishing enterprise, founded by him for
the benefit of the progressive young Russian composers. This
"Édition Russe" helped much to introduce the new Russian music
to other countries. In Moscow he also evolved far-reaching ideas
as an educator, plans frustrated by the first World War and the
Russian revolution, but resumed many years later and realized
in the Berkshire Festivals and Center of music. His active interest in social reforms in the field of music led him to bringing the
art to the masses of the people in the huge domain of Russia. His
fantastic expeditions all along the Volga River, through a
thousand miles to the Caspian Sea, described elsewhere in this
book, illustrate sensationally his boldness, his magnanimous
hospitality, his democratic idealism, and his resourcefulness.

As Koussevitzky approached his fortieth year, he was not only a superior musician and virtuoso of conducting like his associates with the baton in other countries, he was also a leader who stressed the national and international point of view, the mutual interchange of cultural accomplishments. He was a propagator of novel and timely ideas in education. As a publisher, he gave generous support to the creative musicians. As a friend of the common people, he was desirous to transmit the message of great art in a truly democratic sense. In this ensemble of aims and achievements, Koussevitzky was and is more than a foremost professional conductor; in America as well as in Russia, he has been a cultural force of true magnitude.

Turning now to Koussevitzky's individual conception of the art of conducting, his character as an interpreter, and the nature of his art as compared to that of other eminent conductors, we invite the reader to follow us in his imagination to Boston Symphony Hall, to a number of rehearsals and concerts.

The orchestra is normally assembled six times every week. From Monday to Thursday Koussevitzky rehearses daily from ten A.M. to one P.M.; on Friday afternoon and Saturday night two public concerts are scheduled. Formerly a little crowd of favored guests had special permission to attend the Thursday rehearsal, when the entire program of the week's concert had already been painstakingly prepared and a quasi concert-like performance could be expected. These rehearsals were a most interesting, sometimes exciting, experience; and to musically experienced visitors they were most informative in regard to the qualities of the new works especially, the conductor's approach to his task, and the orchestra's response to the demands made on its technical virtuosity and mental alertness. A few years ago, when the Orchestra became a member of the Musicians' Union, this privilege was withdrawn; disappointed friends of the Orchestra were told that the Union objected to visitors at the rehearsal, though it is not easy to see what valid reason the Union had to forbid the presence of a few specially interested guests. At any rate, whether this was the real reason or not, rehearsals ever since have been held in strictest privacy, and one

of the most valuable sources of instruction and experience has
been barred to a number of gifted young students and composers eager to learn. The mechanism of the Orchestra, the
structure of a symphonic score, the technical methods of conducting undoubtedly can be learned better at a rehearsal, with
its interruptions, repetitions, and the critical remarks of the
conductor, than at a polished public performance rapidly gliding
past the ears of the listener.

At ten o'clock sharp Koussevitzky quietly appears at his desk,
usually wearing across his shoulders a soft, dark cape or shawl
which he leaves on a chair near by until he walks out at inter-
mission time or at the close of the rehearsal. For a while the
rehearsal will go on smoothly, then suddenly Koussevitzky may
stop the Orchestra, addressing a brief critical remark to a group
of instruments or to some individual players. These remarks are
made sometimes in English, at other times in French, German,
or Russian, according to the nationality of the persons addressed
—about eighteen nationalities are represented in the Orchestra.
Koussevitzky is not in the habit of giving long, explanatory lectures to his orchestra, as Mengelberg used to do at his Amsterdam
Concertgebouw Orchestra rehearsals, but his brief instructions
are exactly to the point, and one might often be surprised to
notice what an improvement results from such a sharply shouted
order. At other times one might consider a certain phrase quite
effective and correct, finding no reason for dissatisfaction. But
after the passage has been played according to Koussevitzky's
directions, it is not hard to find it much more beautiful in sound
and much more impressive in sentiment. The conductor's sensitive ear, his vast experience and keen knowledge of the most
refined *valeurs* of sound—to use a favorite term of painters—his
sense for the subtlest sonorities, all this ever present in his aural
imagination prompts him to suggest small yet striking changes
that produce surprising effects not present a minute earlier.

At these rehearsals one can perceive the immediate cause of
the Boston Symphony Orchestra's universally acknowledged
eminence, can learn the difference between a satisfactory, "good"
rendering and outstanding orchestral playing. What gives the

Orchestra its unique excellence is not only its superior technical skill—a few other orchestras are in this respect about equal—but also the use made of its technical virtuosity. To exploit the maximum of its playing power even the best orchestra must have a conductor of superior authority and experience, an inspired and inspiring leader able to provoke the individual players to efforts of will power, energy, and exaltation not willingly expended most of the time. It takes a Koussevitzky to extract from the Orchestra that famous Boston fortissimo, brimful of brilliant sonority, strong as a thunderclap, yet flexible and noble in quality of sound; or its counterpart, a pianissimo like a thin thread of shining silk, yet like a nerve vibrant with the breath of life. The velvet-like softness and smoothness of the darkly tinged Boston string section or its radiant brightness, reflecting as it were rays of sunlight—rarest marvels of sound, streaming forth from the elastic bows of its small and large fiddles—have been admired in many cities. The cutting sharpness of its pointed rhythms, suggestive of the swift stroke of a gleaming blade, the vigor and precision of its accents impart a particular zest to the playing of this orchestra. Other distinctive features are the irresistibly brilliant dash, the impetuosity of its *Attacca,* its exciting, dramatic crescendo and accelerando, and at the opposite end of the dynamic scale its languid, sensuous diminuendo and rallentando, the coquettish elegance of its rapid, faint staccati, the swaying grace and alluring feminine softness of its dance melody and accompaniment. These and many other enchanting sound effects would not be heard in equal refinement and perfection without Koussevitzky's constant vigilance and daily training. The Boston Symphony, as it plays at present, is an instrument fashioned to perfection by the abnormal sensitivity of its conductor and trained to respond instantly to his faintest direction. Yet the marvel is that the Orchestra's admirable discipline, its ever present *esprit de corps,* does not result in mechanical perfection but in the appearance of a living organism, fully animated, soulful, persuasive, and intensely interesting to the listener at every moment. This result confronts us with one of the mysteries of creative artistic reproduction and interpretation.

The problem of interpretation is inseparable from the problem of style. How does Koussevitzky react to the demands of the various styles with which he has to deal in his amazingly diversified programs?

His repertory includes the entire current symphonic literature, classical, romantic, and modern, from Vivaldi, Corelli, Handel, and Bach to Stravinsky and the younger American modernists. Koussevitzky himself hardly lays any claim to particular scholarship in the field of musicology. Yet his inborn and long-cultivated instinct for the demands of style is so strong and sure that he invariably grasps the fundamental, essential points, though sometimes paying less heed to formalistic details. He is not in quest of an archaeologically correct return to an antiquated sound ideal, arising from the limited means of the eighteenth-century masters. Having at his disposal the large Boston Symphony Orchestra and the Harvard and Radcliffe choruses with more than three hundred singers, Koussevitzky would not dream of performing Bach's passion music and B minor Mass with the little chorus of about thirty high-school and university students and the tiny orchestra of twenty-five players with which Bach had to content himself because he could not afford to hire better forces. Koussevitzky's interpretation is powerful, and convincing, as it remains true to the spirit of the immortal score. It brings out the greatness of Bach's music, which in Bach's own performance in all probability could not have been revealed to his listeners. Indeed, inadequate reproductive apparatus sufficiently explains why Bach's gigantic works remained totally unknown for a century and more.

While stressing the demands of monumental music in a way contrary to the letter of tradition, Koussevitzky honors tradition when it helps to support the character of the music. Thus he performs Bach's Brandenburg Concertos and orchestral suites in chamber music manner, with a small orchestra, as these compositions with their delicate and involved part leading would lose much of their intimate character by the too-massive sound of a large modern orchestra. Exquisite examples of this Bach chamber orchestra music were presented at the Berkshire Bach-Mozart Festivals in August 1945 and 1946.

For Mozart, too, Koussevitzky has lately preferred a smaller orchestral body. It was especially interesting at the Bach-Mozart Festival to observe how carefully Koussevitzky differentiated the styles of the two masters. In Bach's music he preserved a plastic sound in black and white, so to speak; its dynamic scale derived from the organ style with its terraces of forte and piano, without many intermediate gradations of crescendo and diminuendo. In Mozart's music, he replaced the plastic Bach sound with a much softer, colorful sound, rich in delicate shadings and vibrant with intimate sentiments, the soulful accents of youthful passion, a frequent and rapid change of expression even within the confines of the same theme.

In matters of tempo Koussevitzky has often been criticized for taking the allegro and presto pieces at too rapid a pace, and the slow movements too slowly. This is the most convenient brand of crude criticism. If a critic finds no other valid objection he can always fall back on "wrong tempo." In reality, however, there exists no universally correct and applicable standard of tempo. One may even assert with good reason that for a certain piece two or even three different tempos may be equally right, according to the conception and temperament of the performer, his skill in coördinating the single sections of the piece convincingly, and his technical mastery of playing. When Koussevitzky takes a presto finale of Mozart or Haydn at a much faster pace than a listener has heard formerly, this tempo is right for Koussevitzky and the Boston Symphony Orchestra, because they can control it so well that the music fairly scintillates in a fascinating manner, the fastest passages come out with perfect clearness and apparent ease, and the lightness and gaiety, the humor, wit, and alacrity of the music are perfectly interpreted. The same tempo taken by a less skillful conductor and orchestra will be wrong, the music sounding hurried, labored, and devoid of grace and elegance. In this regard, the author recalls the incomparable pianist Ferruccio Busoni, who used to play the finales of Mozart concertos with an incredible speed, a sparkling virtuosity that brought out the real spirit of this transcendentally gay music in an irresistibly brilliant manner. But Busoni's tempo was right only for him. It would have been wrong and even pernicious for most other pianists.

A great charm of Koussevitzky's style of conducting consists in his free treatment of tempo changes, in his art of using elastic accelerandos or ritenutos as transitions from one tempo to another. Especially in Beethoven's dramatic and pathetic symphonies, in the psychologically complex music of Brahms, Tchaikovsky, Sibelius, and Shostakovich, the flow, convincing coherence, and logical structure depend largely on the conductor's capacity to divine meanings that are written out in the score only approximately, as our system of notation is not subtle and distinct enough to express all emotional and rhetorical refinements. A wide field is open to the conductor's power as an interpreter, but it has its dangers, since the dividing line between a genuine interpretation and one that is fanciful and distorting is easy to miss. Only a phenomenally gifted and highly experienced conductor will move on this dangerous ground with ease and sureness. The cultivated musical public has a flair for such distinctions, and has by its unshakable verdict placed Koussevitzky in the first rank of the great conductors of our age.

Such honors are not quickly won and are awarded only after a long career, full of extraordinary merit and to a personality unique in its class. This promotion to the rank of field marshal in the army of music is fundamentally different from the applause greeting a talented newcomer, who has accomplished one or two sensational feats but has to prove his sterling quality by equal achievements through many years, and who has as much to gain as to lose.

Koussevitzky's truly cosmopolitan attitude is indicated by the fact that it is hardly possible to decide whether he excels more in German, Russian, French, or American music. His Beethoven, Schumann, Brahms, and Richard Strauss renderings could not have been surpassed at Vienna or Berlin when those now ruined cities were at the peak of their musical eminence. In particular,

Koussevitzky's Eroica and Ninth Symphony deserve to be preserved on the best records available in order to show future generations what a great Russian conductor in America was able to achieve with the most sublime German music. No less remarkable is Koussevitzky's Brahms interpretation, combining depth and breadth of conception with nobility and enchanting beauty of sound effect. The so-called rugged Brahms loses nothing of his manly vigor, his densely knit formal structure, his seriousness and greatness, but gains much by Koussevitzky's predilection for the lyric beauty and emotional warmth of the Brahms melody. One might wish that Koussevitzky would offer Bruckner's and Mahler's monumental symphonies more frequently than he has done. The scarcity of appearance of these great Viennese masters on Boston programs may be because of the influence of American critics on the American public. More likely is the explanation that Koussevitzky's constant care for the new American music, plus his self-imposed international obligations, leaves him too little opportunity for adequate study of these complex, pretentious scores. More than once Koussevitzky has shown that he does not accept silently an unjust attack by the critics; and as to his public, he prefers to guide it and to overcome its resistance rather than to yield to its prejudices.

That Koussevitzky has supreme authority in Russian music is naturally expected and believed in America. Whereas he may have three or four close competitors in the rendering of German and French music, it would hardly be possible to name a musician anywhere in America who could successfully challenge him in the performance of Moussorgsky, Rimsky-Korsakoff, Tchaikovsky, Scriabin, Shostakovich, and Prokofieff. Other able conductors in this country reveal the great Russian music only to a certain extent. But Koussevitzky alone sums up all the decisive factors in Russian music and brings fully alive its Slavic soul, with all its fiery passion and depth of unrestrained melancholy, its joyful ecstasies and sensuous ardor, its almost savage force and its rustic humor, its fatalism and quasi-oriental languor. Similarly, Koussevitzky possesses the key giving him access to all heights and depths of the Nordic music of Sibelius. One will hardly ever hear more authoritative and accomplished performances of the Finnish master's music than in Boston. In some ways this symphonic music is affiliated with the Russian art, not as its sister but perhaps as its sister-in-law.

It is doubtful whether at the present time French symphonic music can be heard anywhere, not excluding Paris, played as brilliantly and enticingly as in Boston. Berlioz, César Franck, Debussy, and Ravel, especially the last two, are preferred by Koussevitzky. His long residence and professional activities in Paris, his personal acquaintance with leading French musicians, have given him both intimate insight into the character of the French art of music and sympathy with its aims. Along with Toscanini and Monteux, Koussevitzky has transplanted, at least temporarily, the trusteeship of the great French music from Paris to America. Even more so than for German and Russian music, the utmost refinement of coloristic treatment is indispensable to the perfect rendering of French impressionistic music; and fortunately Koussevitzky has an orchestral group skilled in realizing such an artistic accomplishment.

German, Russian, French, and American symphonic music makes up the bulk of Koussevitzky's programs. He always, however, reserves space for especially interesting works from England, Poland, Hungary, Italy, and elsewhere. In this truly cosmopolitan attitude, Koussevitzky is in advance of all other conductors, not only in America but also in prewar Europe.

In discussing Koussevitzky as an artist, one comes to a matter that is of special interest to the concert-hall public though perhaps not to the professional musician—a matter that can be summed up in the words "public appearance." The professional musician knows that a conductor's principal work with the orchestra is done at rehearsals and that the public concert is, so to speak, a clean copy of an essay fully drafted in advance and corrected in all details. The public, however, believes that the conductor's manner of wielding his baton and his personal appearance and action at the desk electrify the men of the orchestra in some mysterious way and are primarily responsible for the impression the listener receives. There are different types of conductors as they appear before the public: some are handsome, elegantly dressed, carefully groomed men, intent on impressing the audience—especially the ladies—by their *mondaine* aspect. In their style of conducting, too, they stress elegance, beauty of motion, carefully avoiding any aberration in the opposite direction. In his younger years, Arthur Nikisch was the unsurpassable example of this type. Others, unpretentious in their appearance, trust more in the power of their musicianship than in showmanship. Of this type, Karl Muck was perhaps the most accomplished representative: with a minimum of agitated motion he obtained all desired effects, a glance of his eyes and the expression of his face sufficed. Still others act a theatrical part at their desk, gesticulating profusely and violently, transmitting the emotion of the musical score to the orchestra and the public by their own bodily reaction, mindful of the fact that the concert-hall public not only wants to hear the music but also likes a spectacle. Were the conductor to be made invisible to the public as in Wagner's Bayreuth Theater, a great attraction for many people would be lost.

Koussevitzky in a way is a composite example of all these types, assembling various traits with good taste and rejecting gross exaggerations. A man of the world in his distinguished appearance, he yet manifests to everyone that he is still more an artist, passionately intent on his cultural mission. As an advocate for the great art of music, he pleads to the large jury filling the concert hall. Outbursts of passion are restricted to a few, decisive moments, but when they arrive, at the proper place, their effect is irresistible. He also has repose, grace, simplicity, quiet humor, and artless gaiety at his command, and all intermediate expressions on the emotional scale. His manner at the desk is not designed to draw attention to himself but to underline the character of the music, and to encourage his players in giving their best on the spur of the moment.

Finally it may be attempted to define Koussevitzky's position in the small elite of conductors of the very first rank. This exalted class is a small one—in the author's opinion including Toscanini,

Bruno Walter, and Wilhelm Furtwängler, as well as Koussevitzky—with Georg Szell, Otto Klemperer, Erich Kleiber, Rodzinski, Mitropoulos, and two or three others as younger aspirants to highest honors in the reserve. It would be presumptuous to attempt balancing in detail their respective merits and excellences, each one of them having individual greatness. Yet it may not be unjust to assert that of all conductors Koussevitzky is the most universal and cosmopolitan, not only because of his great art but also by reason of the exceptionally independent position he occupies at the head of the Boston Symphony Orchestra. Toscanini, with all his eminent mastery, does not have much interest in American music, preferring Italian symphonic scores, generally considered the less valuable part of the musical productions of Italy, with its center of gravity in opera. Bruno Walter has not had enough independence in America to show the full extent of his powers; he is expected to perform mainly the Viennese classics, Mozart, Haydn, Beethoven, Schubert, and Brahms, with a little Bruckner and Mahler mixed in occasionally—not because his American public demands it, but because of his well-known love for these masters. Furtwängler's eminent art is an almost unknown quantity in America and likely to remain so for political reasons.

Koussevitzky's manifold activities, his international affiliations, and his authority in a multitude of fields are at present unique in America; altogether they represent the maximum of active power and influence ever accorded to a musician in this country.

CHAPTER 14

KOUSSEVITZKY AS
AN EDUCATOR

Our survey of American works performed at Boston has clearly
indicated how deeply the new American music is indebted to
Koussevitzky. Without his ever ready help much of it would not
have been written at all, and many other scores would have
remained unknown and hardly ever performed. Yet his unique
achievements in behalf of American music are not exhausted by
the extensive new literature introduced by him at his Boston
concerts. The new American music, as Koussevitzky sees it, is not
concerned exclusively with what our progressive composers are
doing. They furnish us the substance, the spiritual food, which,
however, must be served to the consumers in a proper dish. For
the establishment of a national school of American music the
manner of its presentation is hardly less important. On this
outward form of our musical life Koussevitzky has very unorthodox, even revolutionary, ideas. They are concerned with the
methods of teaching, with the organization of concerts and opera,
with the financing of music projects, and with the duty of the
government to do its share in the building up and maintenance
of a national art of music.

Many of Koussevitzky's important cultural and educational
aspirations he has realized through the establishment of the
Berkshire Symphonic Festivals and the Berkshire Music Center.
The Festivals are the outcome of an educational idea, and the
Festivals as well as the Center are closely related to the new
American music, the principal theme of this book. The Festivals
aimed at gaining a new, much larger public for the symphonic
art, and the center had as its main purpose the education of
young composers, the future creators of the new American music,
and of able musicians, trained in the modern styles, the future
players and conductors of the new American works.

For a long time Koussevitzky fostered the idea of establishing summer music festivals on a greater and wider scale than any which had so far existed in the United States; they were to be not a copy of those at Salzburg and Bayreuth in the old world, but something adapted to the American atmosphere. It was not until the mid-thirties that his idea gained concrete form. In the town of Stockbridge, in the Berkshire Hills of western Massachusetts, a music festival had been held in 1934, conducted by Henry Hadley with a major part of the New York Philharmonic-Symphony Orchestra, and the enterprise was repeated in the summer of 1935. In 1936 the Festival Committee of the Berkshire organization invited the Boston Symphony Orchestra for a series of three concerts. They met with such resounding success that the Festival Committee resolved to make these concerts of the Orchestra conducted by Koussevitzky a permanent institution. This plan was realized in a manner hardly to be foreseen when Tanglewood, one of the most extensive and beautifully located estates of the entire Berkshire district, was magnanimously presented to the Boston Symphony Orchestra as a permanent home for its summer festivals. The former owners of the estate, Mrs. Gorham Brooks and Miss Mary Aspinwall Tappan, have thereby earned the enduring gratitude not only of the Orchestra but also of uncounted multitudes of music lovers. Festival guests can now enjoy the spacious gardens, fine lawns, and beautiful old trees of Tanglewood—idyllic charms that along with the hospitality of the estate's owners had attracted a number of poets, writers, and authors for nearly a hundred years. Among the illustrious guests entertained by the Tappan family at Tanglewood were Ralph Waldo Emerson, Oliver Wendell Holmes, and Herman Melville; and in a little red cottage once situated in the parklike grounds, Nathaniel Hawthorne had written his famous *Tanglewood Tales* and *The House of the Seven Gables*. The history of the estate and of the foundation of the festivals is pleasantly told in Mr. M. A. DeWolfe Howe's recently published book, *The Tale of Tanglewood*.

The realization of Koussevitzky's festival idea through this generous gift meant that many people living far from the

great American centers of music—New York, Boston, Philadelphia, and Chicago—would have the opportunity of actually being
present to hear great masterpieces of symphonic music played
with perfection by one of the world's most famous orchestras
and conducted by one of the world's most eminent masters. Until this time symphonic art had been known to most Berkshire summer guests only through records and by radio. They
could now experience how far even the best mechanical renderings are behind the actual performance, animated by the enthusiasm and the authority of a great reproductive artist and made
alive by the noble and brilliant work of that unmatched ensemble
of a hundred or more virtuosos known as the Boston Symphony
Orchestra.

How well Koussevitzky's initiative was appreciated by the
public and how closely he had foreseen the reaction of the
public are illustrated by the official statistics of attendance in
the various years. The first festival, in 1934, had attracted approximately five thousand visitors. No precise figures are available for the next season, in 1935. But when Koussevitzky first
took over in 1936, the records show that attendance jumped very
close to fifteen thousand for three concerts. In 1938, attendance
at six concerts reached thirty-eight thousand, and still more
people came in 1939 and 1940, when nine concerts were given
each year instead of six. In 1941 the nine concerts assembled
about ninety-five thousand guests. Proceeds from one of the 1941
concerts were devoted to British War Relief and to a collection
of Boston Symphony Orchestra records that were shipped to
several American camps. The Festival seasons had to be suspended after 1942, as the war greatly restricted automobile
traffic, on which the majority of guests relied. Yet in 1944,
Koussevitzky's plea for a festival on a smaller scale prevailed,
and the series of Mozart works played by a chamber orchestra
of some thirty prominent members of the Orchestra was a de-
lightful experience. For 1945, a Bach-Mozart festival with a
chamber orchestra was given, and in 1946 both the Festival and
the Center were revived in full extent.

The magnificent Tanglewood estate needed considerable adaptation to its new use. During the first years, the accommodations consisted of a wooden shell and plain benches and a big tent that provided insufficient shelter during several rain storms. In 1938, a more substantial auditorium was built, the big Shed, with a capacity of more than six thousand seats. For this structure, more than $80,000 had been raised by voluntary subscription, to which the public responded liberally. The Finnish architect Eliel Saarinen designed the Shed, and Professor Richard D. Fay of the Massachusetts Institute of Technology devised its scheme of acoustics. The Shed was inaugurated on August 4, 1938, at the first concert of the summer season and convincingly proved its fine acoustic qualities. A few years later, when the Music Center had begun to function, need arose for a theater and concert hall seating twelve hundred persons, for the performance of operas as well as concert music; in addition a smaller chamber-music hall and five small studios were required; by 1941 all these new buildings were ready for use. The old mansion, commanding a beautiful view of Lake Mahkeenac with its broad background of mountain scenery, became the central office.

Koussevitzky's festival idea was a variant of one tried out formerly in a number of places in Europe and America. The Berkshire Festivals, however, were triumphant through the fact —well recognized by their many guests—that they surpassed their older competitors in quality. All the works performed during the various seasons belonged to the regular repertory of the Boston Symphony Orchestra and had been heard in Boston and New York. The programs' American scores, already treated in earlier chapters, were E. B. Hill's Sinfonietta, Opus 40a, in 1937; Copland's "Music for the Theatre," in 1938; Piston's Concerto for Orchestra, in 1939; Roy Harris' Symphony No. 3, in 1940; Copland's "Quiet City," Hanson's Romantic Symphony, and Barber's Violin Concerto (played by Ruth Posselt), in 1941; and Hanson's Symphony No. 3, in 1942. Randall Thompson's "Alleluia" was written especially for the inauguration of the Music Center in 1940 and was heard on that occasion. In 1946 Copland's "Appalachian Spring," Schuman's "American Festival Overture," and

Thompson's "The Testament of Freedom" were played. In addition, this season saw the first American performance of Symphony No. 9 by Shostakovich.

Koussevitzky was not content with the valuable services that the Festivals were rendering to the country's music lovers. He recognized that Tanglewood had become an ideal site for a unique educational experiment—a "Center" for advanced musical instruction. The concept of such a center had occurred to him back in 1913 when he was in Moscow, but its fulfillment had been prevented by the outbreak of war in 1914 and the Russian Revolution which followed. Now, when he outlined his concept to the trustees of the Boston Symphony Orchestra, and explained its "meaning in American life and its influence on the arts and culture of this country," the president of that corporation, Mr. E. B. Dane, replied, "Go ahead, we cannot afford to lose it." Thus the Boston Trustees identified themselves with the new enterprise, as the Berkshire Festival Committee, headed by Miss Robinson Smith, had already done with regard to the Festivals.

In the project for what he called "The Berkshire Music Center," the eminent conductor revealed himself also as the possessor of a pedagogical mind with rare clarity of insight into the actual conditions of musical instruction—into its weaknesses, but also into its possibilities of progress. The program as planned and explained by him showed him to be the very rare combination of a daring and enthusiastic idealist and a wise and resourceful realist. To his broad artistic aims he brings the precise knowledge of routine technicalities acquired by a practitioner in long experience. He devised a plan which appeared fantastic at first sight and yet has proved feasible and successful in the four seasons so far held.

Young musicians, admitted to the Center after rigorous tests, were to spend six weeks in summer in daily communion with genuine masters of musical art. They would either be pupils in advanced, well-designed courses for a limited number, or members of general sessions open to all for singing in a chorus, playing in a student orchestra or in chamber-music ensembles,

listening to lectures, attending concerts and rehearsals of the
Boston Symphony Orchestra. In short, here was an opportunity
for intensive musical activities of a variety and excellence not
possible in any music school, where the pupil comes for a lesson
once or twice a week and is left to shift for himself the rest of
the time.

At Tanglewood several hundred aspirants to artistic honors,
young men and women, live in a saturated musical atmosphere
from morning until night. Something interesting is going on all
the time. Great works of symphonic and choral literature become
familiar to the students through a long series of daily rehearsals.
How a finished performance is prepared and gradually built up
is demonstrated in the clearest possible manner. Lectures by
eminent authorities treat historical and aesthetic problems, explain the nature and style of the masterpieces scheduled for
performance. How an opera is put on the stage can be seen by
everybody—a rare experience. Classes in harmony, counterpoint,
composition, in the "principles and methods of teaching music
in schools" are provided. Individual instruction in orchestral
instruments, singing, and piano is also given to those desiring it.

The Music Center in 1940 had two branches, initially called
"A School for Advanced Study," and a "Department of Music
and Culture." The School was intended for smaller groups of
advanced, highly gifted young musicians, the best of many able
and talented applicants. Four departments were open to them:
(1) A class of orchestral conducting, directed by Koussevitzky
and his assistant, Stanley Chapple; (2) an orchestra of advanced
players, who studied in detail and performed a number of symphonic and chamber music works assigned to them, with the
assistance of their instructors, the leading members of the Boston
Symphony; (3) an opera class, under the supervision of Dr. Herbert Graf, the distinguished stage director of the New York
Metropolitan Opera, with Boris Goldovsky as assistant; (4) two
classes in advanced composition, conducted by Aaron Copland
and Paul Hindemith.

The "Department of Music and Culture" was designed for the

bulk of the students not specializing in one of the restricted and advanced studies taught to the small, advanced group in the School. "Constant participation in music through singing or playing" was demanded of every student member of the Center, either in the orchestra—a different body from the School orchestra—or in the chorus. A considerable number of lectures dealt with problems of history, styles and form, music instruction, and so on. In 1940, Olin Downes, music editor of the *New York Times*, gave a course of six lectures on "Music and Integrity," elucidating important aesthetic and ethical questions, and Abram Chasins gave six lectures on the controversial topic of musical ornamentation. Other lecturers in 1940 were Professor Archibald T. Davison of Harvard University; Randall Thompson, then director of the Curtis Institute in Philadelphia; and Augustus D. Zanzig of the National Recreation Association. A course on "Music in the Schools" was given by Howard Abell of Milton Academy. Professor G. Wallace Woodworth, conductor of the Harvard Glee Club, was in charge of the Chorus and of a class in choral conducting. The chief work prepared by the Chorus in 1940 was Bach's B minor Mass, performed as a part of the Festival on August 15, and conducted by Koussevitzky. A unique feature of the Center was that the second half of its term coincided with the Festival, when students had access not only to all public concerts but also to the highly instructive rehearsals held by Koussevitzky with the Boston Symphony Orchestra and the chorus.

The general schedule of 1940 was maintained during the sessions of 1941 and 1942 with some changes in the faculty. Hugh Ross, director of the Schola Cantorum of New York, the famous violoncellist Gregor Piatigorsky, the harpsichordist Putnam Aldrich, Dr. Howard Hanson, director of the Eastman School of Music in Rochester, and Dr. Carleton Sprague Smith of the New York Public Library were newcomers at the 1941 session. Beethoven's *Missa Solemnis* was the great choral work performed at the 1941 Festival. During this season, the Center accommodated three hundred and thirty-eight students, selected from seven hundred and ninety-six applicants. The students came from thirty-four states of the Union and from eight foreign countries.

Interest was naturally centered on Koussevitzky's class in conducting, to which he had admitted only a few particularly talented young men. They enjoyed his special favor and interest. After intensive work with Koussevitzky and his assistant, Stanley Chapple, they had a chance of showing publicly what they had learned. At this test performance Leonard Bernstein (of Harvard and the Curtis Institute), Lukas Foss (Curtis Institute), Richard Bales (Juilliard Foundation), and Thor Johnson (University of Michigan) distinguished themselves. Bernstein and Foss have in the meantime made a name for themselves in their professional work. In the 1941 session six Koussevitzky pupils were loudly acclaimed for their skill in conducting: Leonard Bernstein, Walter Hendl (in 1945–46 assistant to Rodzinski in New York), Thor Johnson, Richard Duncan, Richard Korn, and Robert Whitney.

The composition classes of Copland and Hindemith were also small, restricted to especially gifted students. In 1941 only sixteen young composers were admitted out of forty-six who had applied. For the 1942 season Igor Stravinsky had been announced as presiding master in a course of composition. As he was prevented from attending, his place was taken by Bohuslav Martinu, the noted Czech composer whose name has become familiar to the musical public through a number of new works performed by Koussevitzky.

The opera department, with its nineteen active singing members, performed in 1941 under Dr. Herbert Graf's general direction Mozart's *Così fan tutte,* in English, with two different casts, besides scenes from other operas. Stage settings were manufactured by members of the opera group trained by Richard Rychtarik, and the orchestra was conducted by Boris Goldovsky. In 1942 the opera department gave a very creditable performance of Nicolai's *The Merry Wives of Windsor.* In 1946 the first American performance of Benjamin Britten's new opera *Peter Grimes,* commissioned several years earlier by the Koussevitzky

Foundation, excited uncommon interest. It was conducted by Leonard Bernstein.

The 1942 season differed from its predecessors by the absence of the Boston Symphony Orchestra, owing to wartime restrictions. Koussevitzky, however, insisted on continuing and financing the work of the Center under the authority of the Koussevitzky Musical Foundation, Inc. In this way, there was no lack of symphonic music offered to the public. Koussevitzky assembled a large student orchestra from the best players of many cities. With this new orchestra he himself worked day by day, training it, polishing it, making it obedient to his rigorous demands. After protracted preparation he announced a series of public concerts that proved to be sensational events, a triumph of the conductor's art.

The weight of Koussevitzky's progressive ideas, the magnitude of his personality, have perhaps been best expressed by Robert Lawrence, music critic of the *New York Herald Tribune*, in a report sent to his paper from Lenox on August 10, 1942, after a concert of the student orchestra conducted by Koussevitzky. In it he declared:

> By the results that he has achieved with a student orchestra exactly five weeks old, this conductor must be accounted as one of the greatest cultural figures of our time. . . . Never yet . . . have I heard such a thrilling concert here as that of last night. First of all, it had the spark that can come only from youth—the enthusiasm and receptivity of the young players, who have their careers fresh before them and have not slipped into the deadening ways of routine, and the eternal youth of a conductor whose flame for music has never burned low.

At this concert, Hanson's Third Symphony, Mozart's Concerto for two pianos, and Brahms's E minor Symphony were performed.

A still greater sensation was produced on August 14, 1942, when Koussevitzky conducted a concert for the benefit of Russian War Relief. At this occasion Shostakovich's Seventh Symphony had its first concert performance in America. This symphony, written during the siege of Leningrad and filled with the excitement of that portentous time, had for months been

passionately discussed in American newspapers. The leading
orchestras and conductors of the country had competed for the
honor of the first American performance. Finally Toscanini
conducted the first radio performance and Koussevitzky, with
his student orchestra, the first public concert performance. The
large audience present at this exciting event included Maxim
Litvinoff, head of the Russian Embassy in Washington and
guest of honor; Crown Princess Juliana of the Netherlands;
throngs of distinguished Americans from many cities; and rep-
resentatives of leading American newspapers and magazines.
There was a practically unanimous consent on the excellence
of the performance. The student orchestra surprised all con-
noisseurs by its brilliant playing of the difficult and exacting
score, and Koussevitzky's achievements with the symphony were
enthusiastically acclaimed by the public as well as the press.

The work itself, however, was not so unanimously welcomed
by the critics. Many of them had reservations as to the artistic
value of the score, pointing out what they considered faults of
construction and weaknesses of invention. Koussevitzky, for years
the strongest patron of Shostakovich in America, did not accept
these critical objections silently. By repeated performances, he
tried to refute them. Moreover, in the *Information Bulletin of
the Russian Embassy*, Washington, D. C., August 10, 1942—
entirely dedicated to Shostakovich's Seventh Symphony—Koussevitzky wrote a much-remarked statement defending Shostakovich against the attacks by many American critics. In an interview and in a short essay, "The Simplicity and the Wisdom of
Shostakovich," he compared the young Russian master to
Beethoven:

Shostakovich is the bright torch of the Russian people and its creative forces—inexhaustible as the earth itself. That is why his music is
so overwhelming and human and can be compared with the univer-
sality and humanism of Beethoven's genius, which, like that of Shostakovich, was born in an epoch of world-shattering events. His esthetics may
be considered equal to the esthetics of Beethoven. Having an exceptionally wide scope and freedom of form, which in the Seventh Symphony takes on grandiose proportions, Shostakovich never loses the

feeling of measure, line and unity. His symphony is as solid as granite. In it we see the freedom of the master who has subordinated his instrument to his craftsmanship. In his hand the unyielding granite is sculptured like pliable wax. . . . His music flows from the heart of the creator to the heart of the listener. In this is his simplicity, and in this is his wisdom.

Koussevitzky's apology is revealing not only as regards the nature of Shostakovich's music, but just as much of Koussevitzky's personal artistic convictions. The broadly democratic attitude of Koussevitzky, apparent here as well as on several other occasions, may be surprising to many people having only a superficial acquaintance with his art. To the casual observer he appears to be the most aristocratic and elegant of all conductors, and consequently one credits him with an exclusive love of the most refined and sophisticated, odd music—hence his patronage of ultra-modern music. Yet this conclusion is wrong. The greatest values of music for Koussevitzky lie not in its interesting complications, its feats of virtuosity, but in the strength of the basic human sentiment pervading it, and the radically modern music is valued by him in proportion to the elementary, simple and direct expression of sentiment apparent in it, in spite of its technical complications. This combination of the artistically up-to-date virtuosity with direct, plain human expression attracts him in the music of Shostakovich, and makes him compare it to Beethoven's.

After 1942 the Music Center was compelled to suspend its activities for the duration of the war, as service in the armed forces claimed a great majority of the prospective students. What was achieved, however, during its first three sessions was most gratifying. About one thousand young musicians from all parts of the United States, from Canada, Mexico, Central and South America, and even from a few European countries, participated in the various courses of instruction. In 1946 the activities of the Music Center were resumed, with a faculty personnel largely the same as in former sessions. New names are Robert Shaw, choral conductor, Edward Weeks, editor of the *Atlantic Monthly*, lecturing on music and letters, Professor Irving Fine of Harvard,

Katharine Wolff, for *solfège*, and Boris Goldovsky, conducting the Opera Workshop. On a brief visit at Tanglewood the writer was struck first of all with the joyful energy with which the young students worked at their various assignments, whether at orchestral and choral rehearsals, at lectures, at chamber-music performances, at opera scenes, or in classes of composition. A spirit of exuberance was rampant; a healthy desire to excel animated all these young people, and their enthusiasm knew no bounds. They learned as much as could possibly be learned in the short period of six weeks, owing to the intensity of their work and to the competitive spirit naturally arising in a crowd of young people headed toward a common goal.

But still weightier than their actual technical progress was the broadening of their intellectual and aesthetic capacities, the newly gained insight into the nature of the musical work of art, the influence emanating from the constant intercourse with eminent artists, directing their studies in a friendly, sympathetic spirit. At Tanglewood there was no striving for a degree, no diploma or certificate was given, no examinations were held. Every utilitarian aim was excluded, and most students learned for the first time what a pure artistic, idealistic spirit means—namely the constant striving after perfection, the unadulterated devotion to the artistic task, without admixture of material aims.

Such experiences could not be without their strong imprint on youthful minds. Those thousand Tanglewood students took back to their homes a new, purified artistic spirit, thus spreading it over widely separated regions of the country, fructifying the soil for the growth and production of new artistic ideas. Now that the war is over the Music Center will continue its activities along the directives given by Koussevitzky, and its influence on American music is bound to be considerable, and the master's farsighted ideas will bear fruits which the next generation will gather when they ripen.

The actual achievements of the Berkshire Music Center, however, are only a start on the road to a distant goal. What Koussevitzky has in mind, he expresses as a vision projected into the future; and as early as 1938, when he made preparations for the first session of the Center, he stated in a memorable address to the Trustees of the Orchestra his long-range program. Its essentials, confident and practical, deserve to be quoted:

The United States of America can and are destined to have such a center . . . American freedom is the best soil for it. American financial resources will make it eventually possible. *Rapid growth of American culture dictates its necessity as an historical mission and perennial contribution of America to human art and culture.*

That America, as one of the world's largest and most prosperous countries, has decided obligations to fulfill with regard to the arts, is an assertion that may seem strange and novel to most Americans, who consider art as a private affair of the individual citizen. Here the obligation of Americans collectively, as a nation, is strongly underlined.

Koussevitzky went on to define the ultimate activities of the Center. The symphonic literature, performed by a first-class orchestra is the first and easiest attainable aim. More distant is the second aim: "a series of immortal operas in a perfect ensemble of the finest singers, artists and choruses." Next a series of the most important oratorios and outstanding ballets is promised. More startling is the plan

to give the classical tragedy and comedy with foremost living actors. We expect to recreate the antique Greek theatre in its modern form. For that purpose, leading playwrights, composers, scholars, and other specialists will be invited. Their collective coöperation promises not only a re-creation of the Greek Theatre, but also a creation of a new and great theatrical art, so persistently yet fruitlessly dreamed of by many visionaries of the 19th and the present century.

Coming from the problems of performance to those of teaching, Koussevitzky promises that

the greatest living composers will teach the art of composition; the greatest virtuosi the art of perfect performance; the greatest conductors the mystery of conducting orchestras and choruses. The most eminent thinkers and scholars will lecture there. A free coöperation of such an elite shall certainly result in a creation of new and great values of art; into radiations of the beams of high culture over a nation and the world at large; and finally, into education and training of a new generation of American artists.

All this may sound like a Utopia to the sober American mind. But Bayreuth and Salzburg were also once such Utopias, until the intuition of genius and the constructive skill of eminent intellects succeeded in making them real.

After the Center had actually begun its work in 1940, Koussevitzky in his addresses and manifestoes stressed its immediate aims more than his far-sighted plans for its future. In the 1940 statement he wrote:

We have chosen a practical method so that the students may draw from us some of the essence of the knowledge and experience we have acquired in our years of work.

The 1941 statement read in part:

As music takes its increasing place in the life of America, there is a corresponding desire for a broader comprehension of the art. The Berkshire Music Center offers special opportunities to all for the practice and contemplation of music in its noblest aspects. It brings them into association with the leading artists and scholars of the day. Tanglewood is a place for those who wish to refresh mind and personality by the experience of the best in music and the related arts, and who long for a creative rest in summer.

The central ideas of our short summer work are creation and creative interpretation. Our special aims are to find sound bases for creation and to attain perfection in interpretation.

Obviously, in six weeks we cannot hope to give fundamental courses and instruction on the same basis as they are introduced in conservatories, colleges and music schools. What we want to give our students is constructive advice and a practical method which will stimulate their gifts, round out their abilities gained during their years of study, and broaden their acquaintance with music.

Our problem is to help artists with good training and knowledge to acquire a penetrating and vivid conception of the music they create and interpret; to stir their imagination to new heights and new depths, because imagination invokes in the creator and interpreter the right intuition and emotions to conceive the inner meaning of their art. The fulfillment of this desire, for the time being impossible in Europe, becomes an added obligation in America.

We want to be modest in our promises. But by no means do we want to be modest in our aspiration. We are confident that our students will receive the very best of our ability and practical experience, as well as our spiritual guidance.

These statements are memorable documents in the history of higher musical education in America. One may truthfully assert that even in the old centers of Europe nothing of equal weight and artistic loftiness has ever been offered to a large body of students as a summer course. There have been advanced classes under the guidance of eminent masters in piano, violin, violoncello playing; there have been historical lecture courses, chamber music classes; but nowhere in Europe has there been in one center a world-famous orchestra, a large first-class chorus, an advanced school of composition, and an opera school, in addition to all the features named above.

At the opening of the second season of the Center, in July 1941, Koussevitzky explained the immediate problems more in detail. In his address he singled out two main questions: 1. "How to listen to serious music not as an idle pastime, but so that music will penetrate into the living consciousness of the people." 2. "How and on what basis to establish a fertile and creative contact between youth and their elders in the field of professional musical activity."

In analyzing these basic questions Koussevitzky outlined his philosophy of art. The two problems are so closely linked with each other that it is difficult to separate them. "As practice of the work, and not the theory, is the essence of a living culture, the solutions of these problems can be found only in the process of work itself." In other words, the "appreciation of music," much abused in America, can be obtained only by practical musicianship, by doing things oneself. Reading books and listening to radio, records, and lectures may be helpful, but only in proportion to active musicianship, which they cannot replace.

The aim of the general musical development is to bring the wide masses closer to music, and thereby introduce music into life—not in the accidental manner in which this happens in life, but in a cultural way. . . . General culture in a certain measure plays a more important role than even professional musical education, just because of the participation of the masses which influences the course of culture and the very process of its development.

Koussevitzky further explained that

this problem is new to music and up to now has been little elaborated. It also requires new methods of work because it depends on the sensitiveness of the leaders—professionals—and on their ability to bring music closer to the general public, not through the simplification and impoverishment of art, but remaining at all times on that higher level on which art at the given moment stands.

In order to accomplish this closer approach of the people to the art of music it is necessary "to break down the artificial barriers between the 'initiated' and the 'non-initiated,' in making the musical language as accessible to the general understanding and emotions as is the spoken language." At this point the practical work of the Center begins to function: by its performances, the participation of the students in orchestral and chamber-music playing and in choral singing, the analytical, historical, and aesthetic lectures on musical forms and styles. The essential point is "to introduce into the consciousness of listeners the truly spiritual essence of music which stands high above the level of vulgar amusement and musical diversions."

Koussevitzky believes it will be easier in America to prevent one of the most serious shortcomings of Europe, the detachment of art from the people. To raise the cultural level one must start with the masses of the people. The "problem of general musical education" is of the greatest importance: "The people must be linked with music *organically*, and not merely by an accidental link, based on mutual sympathy or taste. The strength of this link is the guarantee of the entire future growth of music in the country." The work in the general, not exclusively professional, sections of the Center is designed with a view to spreading these cultural, democratic ideas and proving their practical feasibility.

On this "basic layer of musical culture," the spreading of musical understanding among the laymen, professional work must be built up. The professional sphere must be the natural product of the general culture of the people and must "receive living nourishment from it." Otherwise the art of music "will inevitably die off, turning into academism, regardless of whether this may be called classicism or modernism." The conclusion reached by Koussevitzky in his address was that all professional work should tend toward "freedom from any kind of routine and the establishment of a link between musical execution, truly free musical creative work and the living cultural consciousness." The artist, Koussevitzky proclaimed, must "so serve his cause—no matter where and in what capacity—that it be a service to the common work of culture defending it from inner decline and outer destruction. This, then, is true discipline."

Koussevitzky has explained other aspects of his philosophy of art on various occasions, in addresses and interviews. One of the most detailed and revealing interviews may be found in the *New York Times Magazine* of October 19, 1941, written by Howard Taubman. Here we read Koussevitzky's argument that

in a day when the forces of democracy are joined in a showdown struggle with black reaction, music has a tremendous mission to fulfill. It satisfies a spiritual need because it bestows a spiritual power. But what it has to give must be placed at the disposal of the great masses of men and women of America.

He goes on to discuss the problem of music for the masses, a truly democratic art. He is not concerned with what is commonly called "popular" music, good enough for the crowd. For the people, he holds, only the best is good enough. The present organization of our musical life he considers antiquated. The age of wealthy patrons financing orchestras is past. The economic conditions of our present age require a different type of financing. To enable music to fulfill its exalted mission for the large masses of the people it must be brought to the people at the cheapest possible price. By mass attendance, five thousand or more at once, the people themselves may finance an artistic enterprise, though each single visitor pays very little for his ticket. He also points to the need of making the governments—federal, state, municipal—conscious of their duty to support music, concerts as well as opera. He proposes that a small fraction of governmental income through taxes should be diverted to the support of art. Even as small a sum as fifty cents or a dollar a year from each taxpayer would go a long way toward financing concert music and opera for the people.

He has also repeatedly advocated the idea of self-help in the musical profession in the form of a small tax imposed upon its members by large organizations such as the Union of American Musicians. In the *New York Times* of Sunday, May 16, 1943, he published an extended and eloquent article entitled "Justice to Composers," in which he pointed out that of all professional musicians the composers of serious music, with rare exceptions, get the least financial return from their creative work. He advocates the collection of a large fund for the purpose of supporting every year a number of needy and gifted composers:

The appeal for the composer must embrace the whole musical world, reach the musician in every field, the music lover and sponsor, far and wide. It calls for the invaluable support of great music federations; for the joint coöperation of organizations and institutions vitally active in musical life; for the widespread response of all those who derive enjoyment and inspiration from music. . . . We musicians must be first to stand by the composer because we owe him most.*

As yet there has been no great response to this appeal, and it may be expected that Koussevitzky will have to repeat his demand. Yet the Metropolitan Opera of New York made an appeal to the lovers of opera, and collected a large amount of money in small contributions of one dollar each.

Persistence is one of Koussevitzky's characteristic traits. Rarely

* In the same issue of the *New York Times*, Mr. Olin Downes published an extensive commentary on Koussevitzky's article under the heading "Creative New Deal." It expounds general principles that should animate approach to living composers.

if ever does he abandon an idea which he finds useful and necessary. He has the patience to wait for things to mature. He fights
for his plans if necessary, but he also knows that repeating a
plea several times in conspicuous places may finally force people
to pay attention.

His address to the students at the opening of the new session
of the Center in 1946 is a most remarkable document, impressively presented in lucid form. We meet here again his favorite
ideas, in a variant that gives them added force. He stresses especially the mission of art in "the colossal task of world reconstruc-
tion." He complains that "none of the democratic governments
are concerned with this vital question—the subsidy of the arts—
especially musical art." . . . "Art needs the support of the state
and demands a Department of the Fine Arts." But also—and this
is an especially important point—

the state needs art for the purpose of fortifying and completing its
present structure. In ignoring the arts the state will inevitably lose the
sustaining interest and influence of the foremost minds and the creative
spiritual forces of the nation. . . . Is the welfare of a country determined by its magnificent buildings, bridges and roads? Does the happi-
ness of a people depend on economic security and good living alone?
Our world is hungry for spiritual food! But what has been done by our
government to satisfy this hunger? Is there a law preventing democratic
governments to support the fine arts? . . . To-day, in a period of an
unprecedented crisis in history, when men find no common contact and
means of understanding each other, when all nations and values have
lost their former significance, music is an element of unity among men.
More than any other art, music has the driving force, the facility and
freedom of crossing social, political, geographical, racial and religious
barriers, and speaks a language accessible to all. . . . Music alone can
still tame the beast in man—it is our comfort and hope.

It may appear paradoxical that it was a Russian artist who
first pointed out clearly America's obligations to the international art of music and, even more than that, did something
about them—putting timely, novel, and lofty ideas on musical
education into practice. On closer inspection, however, one will
perceive that a great artist with a European background was

needed for this job, a man with a truly cosmopolitan spirit, who also, by long residence and professional activities in this country, had acquired an intimate knowledge of the American musical scene, and who had proved himself a sincere and benevolent friend of new American music. The more closely one looks into the purposes of the Berkshire Festivals and the Music Center, the more clearly one sees that Koussevitzky was the only person in America with sufficient authority, influence, and power for the job not only of conceiving such fruitful and novel ideas, but also of realizing them on a practical basis.

It is a fairly well-established fact that the donation of Tanglewood was a direct consequence of the exceptional authority enjoyed by Koussevitzky, of the confidence inspired by his dynamic personality. The donation of Tanglewood to the Boston Symphony Orchestra actually meant the Boston Symphony Orchestra led by Koussevitzky. The considerable sum needed for the upkeep of the Center, the construction of new buildings, and the establishment of scholarships were also subscribed mainly in consequence of Koussevitzky's personal influence. His many friends and admirers showed their trust in his plans with liberal financial support. Private individuals and institutions like the Eastman School of Music in Rochester, the Curtis Institute in Philadelphia, and the Baldwin Piano Company are found in the lists of subscribers, as well as the Rockefeller and Carnegie foundations, and the ASCAP organization. This broad support, coming from many sources in the American world of music, art, and scholarly pursuits, indicates what hopes have been raised by Koussevitzky's successful initiative.

As an eminent interpreter of the classical and romantic literature Koussevitzky carries on the great traditions of the past. As the friend and helper of modern music he encourages the aspirations and achievements of the present. In his outstanding work as an educator he points to the future, leaving a precious legacy to the generations which are to come.

Koussevitzky's artistic program, containing clear definition of the methods by which it should be executed, and having proved its validity by actual trial, is without parallel. Nevertheless, it is

Koussevitzky's thought on what incentive should guide the men who adopted this program that above all else wins him respect.

The only ground for our authority is the love for us and for our work; and if this were absent, all else would be futility and emptiness —however well we might be "armed" with knowledge and skill.

The undying glory of Beethoven and Bach is based not on their technique and skill, which the public neither knows nor understands, but on the great and inexhaustible love for these men.

But for such love to be able to arise it is necessary first of all that we ourselves do not smoulder like dying embers, but are aflame with sacred love for that which we serve, and those whom we serve—that is to say, for living art and living men.

INDEX

Abell, Howard, 177
Achron, Joseph, 77, 78, 88
Aldrich, Putnam, 177
Americanism in music, 11, 13, 29, 31 (Hill), 38 (Thompson), 41–42 (Hanson), 54–55 (Gilbert), 61 (Converse), 116 (Piston), 127 (Copland), 130 (Harris), 144 (Gould)
American music, 1, 10–12 (definition, historical sketch), 29 (folklore)
Antheil, George, 155
Anthology, Greek, 24
Apollinaire, Guillaume, 90
ASCAP organization, 190
Atonality, 112, 141

Bach, Johann Sebastian, 158, 164, 177
Bach, Philipp Emanuel, 18
Bailly, Louis, 94
Baldwin Piano Company, 190
Bales, Richard, 178
Balokovic, Zlatko, 67
Barber, Samuel, 34, 75, 141–143, 152, 174
Barcelona, 9
Barlow, Howard, 97, 116
Bartók, Bela, 12, 151
Barzin, Leon, 118
Bayreuth, 184
Bedetti, Jean, 83
Beethoven, Ludwig van, 37, 101, 166, 170, 177, 180
Bennett, Robert Russell, 58, 70

Berezowsky, Nicolai, 88, 91–95, 144, 151
Berkshire Festival, 25, 114, 126, 132, 152, 160, 165, 171, 172 (foundation), 173 (attendance), 174 (new buildings), 174–175 (programs), 190
Berkshire Music Center, 7, 38, 148, 150, 160, 171, 173 (purpose, attendance), 182 (students' life and activities), 190 (financial basis)
Berlin Philharmonic Orchestra, 6
Berlioz, Hector, 15, 27, 168
Bernstein, Leonard, 75, 77, 126, 129, 148–150 (Jeremiah Symphony), 152, 178
Biggs, E. Power, 59, 122
Billings, William, 109
Bliss, Arthur, 18
Bloch, Ernest, 12, 34, 37, 52, 77, 78–87, 79 (Viola Suite), 80 (Concerto grosso), 81 (Trois Poèmes Juifs), 83 (Schelomo, America), 85 (Macbeth), 86 (Violin Concerto), 87 (Israel), 112, 151, 152
Blue Network, 136, 145
Borodin, Alexander P., 9, 160
Boston Evening Transcript, 14, 16, 20, 49, 59, 82
Boston Globe, 19, 41, 124
Boston Herald, 15, 16, 19, 55, 123
Boston Post, 20
Boston Symphony Orchestra, 4, 5 (its history, conductors), 152–155 (Fiftieth Anniversary Celebration), 160 (rehearsals), 162–163 (artistic excellence)